DOING BUSINESS WITH BENEDICT

*The Rule of St Benedict and
business management:
a conversation*

Kit Dollard
Anthony Marett-Crosby, OSB
Abbot Timothy Wright, OSB

Illustrated by
Hannah Garland

continuum
LONDON • NEW YORK

CONTINUUM
The Tower Building, 11 York Road, London SE1 7NX
370 Lexington Avenue, New York NY 10017-6503

First published 2002

British Library Cataloguing-in-Publication Data
A catalogue record for this book is available from the British Library.

ISBN: 0-8264-5689-8

Note: The characters mentioned in the case studies are fictitious, and any resemblance to
any person, living or deceased, is entirely coincidental.

Typeset by Kenneth Burnley, Wirral, Cheshire
Printed and bound in Great Britain by Bookcraft (Bath) Ltd, Midsomer Norton

Contents

Introduction:
What's it all About?

Kit Dollard

We are an improbable team: a Catholic layman with a growing family, alongside a young monk of scholarship, and a middle-aged abbot responsible for a large, talented and diverse community of monks, whose ages spread from the second to the ninth decade.

Kit Dollard was educated at Downside and Sandhurst. After ten years in the army serving in Cyprus, Berlin and Northern Ireland (where he was mentioned in despatches), he joined Charles Barker City, the financial PR and advertising agency. He was promoted to Director and was involved in the financial marketing of the privatization of some of the national industries of the Thatcher era (BAA, British Aerospace, British Gas). He won two industry awards for his work with listed companies. At 40, he moved to be Head of Marketing at Strutt & Parker, a firm of chartered surveyors, where he also took on the role of training. Before turning 50 he left the world of business and now he and his wife, Caroline, work collaboratively with the monks at Ampleforth Abbey running a retreat house, courses and workshops. He still works on a regular consultancy basis for a number of professional service firms, as well as coaching individuals in Human Resources and career management skills.

Anthony Marett-Crosby, OSB, was educated at University College, Oxford where he read History. He became a Benedictine monk in 1990 and was solemnly professed in 1995. From

1994 to 1998 he read Theology at Oxford and gained a Doctorate in 2000. He is leader of the Pastoral Services Team and leads retreats and adult formation programmes at Ampleforth and elsewhere. He is the author of books on Monastic Spirituality and History, and admits to knowing nothing about management.

Abbot Timothy Wright, OSB, is the Abbot of Ampleforth Abbey. The third of four sons of an East Midlands businessman and a monk for nearly 40 years, he has been based at the Abbey for all of that time. For 25 years he worked in the school, as teacher of Geography and Religious Studies, then Head of Department, Housemaster and Deputy Headmaster. In the years immediately prior to his election as Abbot in 1997 he was appointed fundraiser for the Abbey and College. He is now half-way through his eight-year term. He has no formal qualifications to be Abbot or to write about management.

This book is a conversation

We want this book to be a true conversation, a conversation in which the reader starts *'with a willingness to emerge a slightly different person. It is always an experiment, whose results are never guaranteed. It involves risk. It's an adventure in which we agree to cook the world together and make it taste less bitter'* (Theodore Zeldin). We are sure that this is just the beginning of an exchange of ideas. Like any conversation, it is a process of listening, reflecting and then responding. Like any good conversation too, it is rarely finished: it can be continued and picked up again later.

There are a number of people in this conversation: ourselves, Benedict through his Rule, various business-writers through their works, practising business people through the case histories, and, most importantly, you, through your own response, reflection and contemplation.

What this book is not about

This book does not provide answers – it is not a 'How to' book. It is not written for monks or nuns neither is it to help 'religious' people in business. It is not an 'academic' book and it does not seek to teach the Rule of St Benedict. We do not claim to be saying anything scholarly or innovative about the Rule itself, about which innumerable expert commentaries already exist. Nor are we claiming that any one religious community has all the answers – far from it.

Our hopes for this book

We have three hopes for this book. Our first hope is that this book offers the opportunity to rise above the violence and fear of the workplace. We hope that it will affirm and encourage you to rise above the 'daily grind' of work and, in doing so, change you and those around you. We believe that many in the workplace are yearning for something more than just promotion, a bigger car, and a holiday home.

Our second hope is that this book will encourage the visibility of Christians in the world of work. The statistics show that 10 per cent of the population admit to being practising Christians, but the reality is that they are almost invisible in the workplace. We hope that this book may challenge you to seek greater integration in your working life, of work and spirit, of body and soul: it is about achieving a balance in life.

Finally, this book is about relationships and real people. It contains, in Benedict's own words, 'nothing harsh or burdensome' and it is ultimately about establishing the priorities and values in life. It is written for anyone who needs inspiration and a vision for themselves or for those they have responsibility to lead. We hope this book will affirm your past, challenge what you do today and inspire you in the future.

A word about style

In our conversation we have grouped our topics under six questions:

1. Is this a conversation I can take part in?
2. What sort of boss should I be?
3. Can I work in this business?
4. Can I improve my working relationships?
5. How can I keep a cool head in a changing world?
6. Where has our conversation arrived?

So we are engaged in a dialogue – we don't have the answers. However tempting it might be to impose solutions, we hope that you will be stimulated to reflect and respond in your own way and in your own situations.

A word about monks

If you have never met a monk or visited a monastery, a thumbnail sketch may help you understand what follows a little more easily.

One way of defining a monk is as 'a rebel on two fronts'.

First of all he is a rebel because he has left his family and friends to seek God. To take such a step today, the individual needs to be independent-minded, even adventurous, because he gives up so much that is taken for granted; he has no freedom to choose what he does, no power of ownership, no freedom to be intimate with a loved one. The monk is a rebel against all that.

The monk is also a rebel in another sense. The attraction of monastic life flows from an experience over which he has little control. We might say he has 'fallen in love with God'. Aware, sometimes acutely so, that his life to date has paid too little attention to God, he seeks a way of rectifying this, by turning his back on his present life to put God first. He is a rebel against the instincts of his own nature.

In the monastery he finds a rhythm of life which, over years, channels this rebellion. The young monk – the double rebel – still lives with the uncertainty of his decision. He misses family and friends and he becomes aware of the fallibility of his temperament. Weakness is not transformed overnight – it is a lifetime's work.

As he progresses, the double rebel learns to accept himself, face his rebelliousness and keep cheerful in spite of everything. The 'cheerful rebel' accepts a new relationship with family and friends, and the need to be weaned of his rebelliousness against God. He realizes, with a sigh of relief, that God, his Abbot and his Community accept him as he is and love him as he is. There is no need for anger.

The monastery is made up of these 'cheerful rebels'; they make it attractive because they offer different perspectives on life, provide lessons in how to build community and show how the most unlikely people can live under the same roof. That will become clear as the book progresses.

Now let's begin.

*Is this a conversation
I can take part in?*

1

Opening Words

Kit Dollard
Anthony Marett-Crosby
Abbot Timothy Wright

Let Business have the first word: what's it like working in business today?

First there is the power. The business world now leads human endeavour. It was not always like this, but the power has shifted. Medicine, the Arts, Science, Sport and Education have all become subservient to businesses or industry in the shape of sponsorship, patronage, partnership or joint ventures. This development has happened so stealthily that many people do not realize it at all. With this change has come a gradual, and in some cases reluctant, realization of the responsibilities that come with this power. For example, many first-world company boards are more powerful than many governments of third-world countries.

Second, there is the speed and nature of change. Most of it, although not all, is driven by technology. A social historian looking back over the last decade of the twentieth century and the first few years of this decade will be amazed at the developments that took place in business. Although there may be discussion over the nature and significance of changes, there will be no argument over either the pace or the stresses and strains that this has imposed on people in work. This is, and will continue to be, the front line.

Tom had been a Senior Partner in a medium-sized firm of solicitors. He was successful by any standard – a leader in his field, much in demand by his clients – yet he had found the last ten years the most difficult of his career, for his gifts seemed at odds with his personal life and desires. He found that too much had changed and that on some days he was no more than a superior office manager. After a particularly bad year, he took early retirement and after a sabbatical when he had time for reflection decided to donate his working time to fundraising for a small third-world charity. It was challenging work but he found it the most rewarding work he had ever done. 'There are only so many times you can go round a golf course' he told his former Partners. 'At last I am doing what I really want. I regret not leaving the old firm earlier.'

In today's business world, people, like products, have become more disposable. The phrase 'bottom line' is common speech in Human Resources (HR) departments where an employee's worth is frequently rated by financial criteria. Mission statements or customer care programmes strive to raise the profile of individuals and businesses, but all too frequently this is just marketing hype, bearing little resemblance to reality.

Many people in business today feel a loss of identity and values. Work can become an all-encompassing commitment, allowing few other interests. This can result in a sense of fragmentation and disjointedness. Work and the rest of life can get out of balance. Sometimes we can become two totally different people, and relationships frequently take second place. Traditional human values become forgotten without being replaced with anything else of value. More than ever, people are saying 'Is this all there is?' Young men in particular seem to be striving to find a sense of identity. For example, we ask, 'What do you do?' or 'Who do you work for?' when perhaps we should be asking, 'Who are you?' Should our work identify what sort of person we are?

Lucy is 31 and has worked for a pharmaceutical company as a junior manager for the last eight years. She enjoys an exciting lifestyle, is paid well and wants for nothing. She has now been selected for the next stage of promotion and offered the chance of attending a year-long, company-sponsored MBA (Master of Business Admistration). The problem is that she must sign a commitment to stay with the company for a further three years. By then she will be 35, and to her horror realizes that she will be middle-aged. Deep down she is worried about the ethics of some company practices and besides, she never quite expected to have a career in this industry. Because of the pressures of the job, she has become ill and finds it hard to see beyond the daily grind of work. She has found that work has lost its enjoyment 'and really, what is the point?'

There is a lack of security in work. Jobs are not for life. Clergy, surgeons, teachers all face the reality that next year their contract may not be renewed. The old careers and lifestyles are changing fast but subtly, and it is not always with the employees' best interests at heart. Frequently change can be brutal and nasty without any vision for the dignity of the human being. 'If you are not part of the solution, you are part of the problem' is a style of management that has its supporters.

But it is not all gloomy news. Expectations are changing. Many graduates, rather than rushing into a career after university, are choosing to take a variety of jobs in different

Should our work identify what sort of person we are?

industries. This gives them a network of contacts and experience across a wide spectrum of businesses so that when they settle for the right job they have excellent contacts. In addition, the concept of a 'career portfolio' is now accepted as a wise way of making progress up the business ladder, as well as providing a more balanced life.

> William is 19 and uncertain about what career to follow. 'I am starting a law degree next year but this year I am learning to be a plumber, taking an NVQ and travelling to Africa where I will be putting my skills to use in helping to reconstruct a hospital. I think our generation is more altruistic than yours. What is the value in making 10,000 more widgets a year? I want to be useful, and by getting two skills I know I will have more chance of doing that.'

There is an almost tangible searching for truth, for something more than the daily grind, by many of today's youth. There is certainly more pressure to succeed. In the developed world, Maslow's hierarchy of needs (with self-actualization at the pinnacle of the triangle) has come home to roost, but this self-actualization now comes with a very practical element.

Now how does Benedict fit in to this, and how can he be relevant to the people of business today?

The Rule of Benedict and its place in history

The Rule of Benedict was written for a group of monks; that is, men who had come together to live a life of prayer and community ordered towards the search for God. But Benedict did not invent the idea of monks and monasteries. In fact, he comes after a long history of development, and the beginnings of what we now call monastic life were ancient history even in Benedict's own day. In the late third and early fourth centuries, 'wild' men and women began to live a strange life in places remote from civilization. These were lonely searchers after God, undertaking this task mainly in prayer, which meant both silent encounter and the praying of the scriptures, but also in manual labour. Some of these men and women truly lived alone, but others came together to form communities. Once communities came into being, so did rules, guidelines for the proper conduct of this new kind of institution. These early rules contain a mixture of detailed regulation and broad principle – on the whole, the regulations have changed, but the principles have remained remarkably constant.

Benedict was the collator of this vast, unwieldy, and at times perilous, tradition. He began as the classic college dropout, abandoning his studies in Rome and fleeing to the wilderness with only his nanny for company. He underwent a series of difficult changes of life, including a period as head of a community who disliked him so much that they tried to kill him by giving him poisoned wine to drink. He probably wrote his Rule late in life, bringing together the monastic tradition with his own experience. So the Rule is the product of the wise Chief Executive, who has learnt much on his journey through life but who has remained stubbornly committed to guiding principles that inspired him in his youth. He believed that these principles would enable his followers to deal with change. He forms out of this a single document, comprising 75 brief chapters. Like the rules that came before it, much of Benedict's writing is concerned with detail, regulations about food and clothing, and sleep and work. But at the heart of the Rule there is a vision, and that is what we are trying to communicate.

It is not easy to say exactly when Benedict wrote this Rule. He was probably born around the year 480, so we guess that it existed by the year 530. What we can say with certainty is that neither Benedict nor anyone else could have guessed the effect that his Rule was to have. Yet its impact upon the later history of Europe has been vast. The Rule is not simply a survivor, but can claim to be part of the cement of Christian culture. By the ninth century, Benedict's Rule was the most dominant guide to religious life, and though other Rules and founders have contributed much to Christianity since, Benedict still holds a special place. For some 1,500 years, men and women have been trying – and no doubt more or less failing – to live up to what it is trying to say.

Since Benedict's Rule is sufficiently flexible to allow for a variety of interpretations, Benedictines, Cistercians, Carthusians and a host of other monastic groupings have each found their own way of living according to Benedict's precepts, each taking Benedict's counsel that things should be arranged in different monasteries according to the demands of particular circumstances, work or cultures. This breadth of vision, this ability for each individual monk to see beyond the walls of his own monastery, is part of the reason why the Rule has survived so long.

But much more important is the enduring value of the way of life he lays out. So today, the Rule is followed by men and women throughout the world, in a huge variety of different cultures. Benedictine men and women undertake a staggering range of work, from making wine to running universities, schools and parishes. The Rule has also attracted large numbers of lay men and women, who see in it something which can make sense for their own lives.

From this we can conclude with a simple point – there is something about the Rule of Benedict that works. Men and women have lived, prayed, worked and even shared their joy together for many years under its inspiration: Benedict's Rule not only brings people together, but somehow enables them to stay together. Perhaps many of you who are reading this will know how difficult that can be.

The vision

So, we come to the vision itself. Simply put, this is what Benedict is trying to do – *to offer an understanding of how a community composed of real people can live and work and pray together, sharing a common search for God.*

Read that again, and ask yourself – is there not something in such a vision which might be worth discovering, putting into practice in our homes, our workplaces and indeed our whole lives? Let us explore the content of this vision for a moment.

The emphasis on 'real people' is important. Benedict never describes monasteries as clubs where saints share their perfection together. This is not what a monastery is at all, despite the impression that we like to give. Saint Benedict describes a monastery by an altogether different metaphor, that of a school. At the beginning of the Rule, he declares:

> So we intend to establish a school for the service of the Lord. (Prologue)[1]

A school is a place where people learn, not a place to which they come, having all the answers.

Notice also the phrase in our definition, 'live and work and pray'. Benedict has no time for some idealized world of men and women living in the ethereal contemplation of their navels. Of course, Benedict's community is founded on prayer, but it is also based on work and community living. A monastery is not a place to which people flee when they cannot face the pressures of work or the demands of living with other people whom they don't much like.

Finally, notice the phrase in our definition, 'search for God'. This summarizes what a monastery is for, as Benedict makes clear in his chapter on the discernment of new recruits:

The first concern must be whether the novice truly seeks God. (RB 58)

In none of the chapters that follow is this spiritual dimension forgotten, for it is this common desire for God which brings followers of the Rule together, and enables them to overcome the difficulties they face. But that search for God has to take place in a context, and it is those practical outworkings which will be our main concern. Prayer is hugely important, but we think there are insights that Benedict has to offer for everyone, including those who cannot or do not pray. The Rule is all about relationships, about one person getting on with another and working with a third and taking orders from a fourth and welcoming the interruptions of a fifth, and praying with and for them all. In this sense, a monastery is like any other community, and it is the working of that community which will be the subject of our dialogue.

Before we can move on, we need to note just three very important principles that underpin the whole of Benedict's Rule.

1. Knowing what not to say

The Rule of Benedict is short – shorter than many of the other comparable texts written at around the same time. Instead of offering lots of detailed rules, Benedict presents, first, a general principle, sometimes supported by an oblique reference to his personal experience. After giving the principle, he then hands over much of its practical application to the local Superior, often with the warning that local circumstances might require some special consideration. Here is an example, much quoted by monks, from the chapter on the proper amount of drink to be provided:

Local conditions or the nature of the community's work or the heat of summer may suggest that a more liberal allowance of drink is needed by the community. In that case it lies with the superior to decide what is needed to meet these conditions. (RB 40)

In all sorts of situations, Benedict provides working examples of delegation when he emphasizes that only the manager on the spot can determine what is an appropriate interpretation of a particular principle. In this, Benedict shows himself far wiser than many of his successors. It is the first element in the model of management by discernment that he creates – knowing what not to say.

2. Being fair

Like anyone who is responsible for a group of people, Benedict wants the management of daily affairs to be marked by fairness. This is his recipe for avoiding the insidious undermining of community life that he calls murmuring. But for Benedict, fairness is not the same as equality. This is fundamental, because he looks on people as different, one from the other. Each has his own needs, his own strong and weak points, and Benedict expects his leaders to be aware of this and to act accordingly.

A simple example concerns differences of age. This is something which any leader, however ignorant of other, more subtle distinctions between people, should be able to notice. On several occasions in the Rule, Benedict reminds his Abbots that the instinct to be fair must be guided by what is proper to the different needs of the young and of the old. So he establishes the principle that:

There is a proper way of dealing with every age and every degree of understanding, and we should find the right way of dealing with the young. (RB 30)

This is hardly a radical or innovative concept. Benedict is making the obvious point that the needs of young and old differ, and argues that equality of distribution must be tempered by this sort of concern.

But it cannot stop there. Fairness to individuals demands a deeper understanding of what drives them, what repels them, and where their limits lie. With the issue of food and drink especially, Benedict reminds his Abbots that one person's favourite dish for a celebratory lunch is another person's opportunity for fasting.

In Sister Sarah's community, it was the ancient tradition that, on every feast day, the community should eat roast duck. No one could really remember why, but it was always produced at Christmas, Easter and other times. Sister Sarah found an overcooked half of duck to be about the worst meal possible, so she did not look forward to those important times when the community ate and celebrated together. People noticed her long face and criticized her for not being a 'good community person'. Then someone thought to ask her why, and she explained that she just couldn't share a celebration over that particular dish, 'But sister', she was told, 'everybody likes duck on a feast day.'

Benedict's response to this kind of human difficulty shows us what fairness towards others really means. In Chapter 39, on what the community should eat, Benedict lays down that:

Two cooked dishes on every table should be enough to allow for differences of tastes so that those who feel unable to eat from one may be satisfied with the other. (RB 39)

If this sounds like an excuse for overindulgence, then you probably like duck! Benedict is not saying that everybody should eat from both dishes, but rather is making the point that the management of daily practical issues should be informed by the remembrance of the differences between people. This is being fair – it is also opening our eyes to those around us.

3. Finding the balance

The word 'balance' is often used of the Rule of Benedict. In his organizing of the day, he shows himself aware of that simple human need to apportion time sensibly and avoid doing the same thing for hours on end. In this, Benedict was helped by the ancient tradition of Jewish and Christian prayer, tied to particular hours of the day: night-time, morning, the hours of the day, and evening. He uses this to establish a series of hinges, points at which his people put one thing down and start something else. So he creates the opportunity for a balanced day, in which the needs of work, the call to prayer, private reading and time with one another all find their place.

This is evident in his discussion of the work done by the community. Benedict's monks are not meant to be idle, but equally he does not lay out in the Rule a charter for work-aholics. He states an important principle when he enjoins on his superiors:

> There must always be moderation in whatever demands are made on the community to protect those who have not a strong constitution. (RB 48)

This kind of implicit distinction between people could be used to distinguish between successes and failures, 'worker bees and drones'. This is precisely the opposite to that which

Benedict intends. He wants the day to be structured so that there are no 'also rans', since he knows that any such judgement serves immediately to exclude and to label.

In case you think that this is all very easy, but just theory, remember the kind of work that Benedict is talking about. He says in the same chapter that monks should live 'by the work of their hands', which in Benedict's own time meant that their daily food depended upon their cultivation and harvesting of crops. So this is not work incidental to the business of survival. It is evident that it is in the context of work that Benedict wants to preserve this balance.

Once again, this depends upon somebody noticing that people are different. Benedict approaches this issue directly in a chapter where he envisages a situation where a monk might be asked to do something that is simply beyond him. All of us, whether leaders or led, know what that feels like. We can justify it as character building, as 'good for him', and satisfy our own guilt by thinking we are doing the person a favour. That is not what Benedict thinks at all. He offers two principles with regard to such a situation, which are intended to be held in balance.

The first is an acceptance of the task given, out of respect for the one who gives it and out of a willingness to see in the leader someone who has concern for the person as well as for the task. There is no room in the Rule for a proud refusal, but rather an openness to the good intentions of those who manage. But at the same time, the one who opposes the task is commanded to listen. The overburdened monk is required to find the opportunity to tell his Abbot that the task is really beyond him. This is not a tidy solution favouring one side over the other: it is an attempt to preserve the balance between the task and the needs of the person who is doing it:

> it would be quite right to choose a good opportunity and point out gently to the superior the reasons for

thinking that the task is really impossible. If the superior, after listening to this submission, still insists on the original task, then the junior must accept that it is the right thing, and with loving confidence in the help of God obey. (RB 68)

*   *   *

The Abbot reflects

Working with people is exciting, unpredictable and frustrating. Some like it, some don't; some are good at it, some are not. So much depends on personality: good managers like working with other people; bad managers see the other as a threat. No manager is perfect; there is always room for improvement. We hope to show how Benedict challenges all our thinking.

Working with people is like handling fragile antique glasses; if you drop one, it makes an awful mess, and can be very expensive. When a manager makes a mistake, it, too, can leave an awful mess, spread resentment and cost a lot of money. Wherever we are, it is in the interests of all to take the matter seriously; to give the way we care for people priority, indeed the highest priority, in our businesses and in our communities.

Kit, in his opening paragraphs, offers us five perceptions which may give a negative sense of business. He suggests it is about power over, rather than empowering; about making products in spite of, not because of, those who work in production; about earning profits rather than building community. Add to this the rate of change, and we see how difficult it is in business for managers both to take decisions to keep ahead of the market and have a good reputation as a company caring for all its employees.

Down the ages there have been outstanding managers of businesses, large and small, who have developed a real sense of community among the employees. I remember one businessman telling me the ideal size of a factory is 350 employees; he was upset he had allowed one of his plants to grow to 800. The point he makes is that friendly relationships within a business are as important for productivity as for the well-being of the employees.

It is also true that, however useful the Rule of Benedict is, we don't have to read far in the history of monasteries to meet both bad Abbots and good Abbots; Abbots who have been very holy, but poor administrators, Abbots good as administrators but poor examples of the search for God. To keep a sense of perspective, all of us, leaders in business and Abbots in monasteries, should reflect on the task we do. That is what this book is for. Only recently has anyone thought of this, but it is an indication how the walls separating people have lowered. We offer, rather tentatively, some reflections on the Rule, and business has a positive role in this conversation.

The key to any organization is the leader. An experienced abbot once said: '*to animate and give life, you must make yourself present, but not omnipresent*': wonderfully true, but difficult to put into practice. The newly installed Abbot, like, I imagine, the newly promoted manager, wants to know what is happening and feel he is in control. It takes time to learn the tricks of the trade.

In the monastery the brethren need space to grow, they need time to make mistakes and to feel trusted. With space, men and women grow and flourish as they develop. The monastery is, after all, a place where a person should grow. Tasks given, even if humdrum and boring, are part of community life, important ways of offering service to others. The monk should be appreciated for these boring tasks, monotonous as they usually are! If he is, he will come alive, grow taller, feel his contribution is important. If the Abbot is behind every pillar, checking up or watching for every false move, then the monk will shrink; he will retreat into his shell, lose his self-confidence and think himself unappreciated and untrustworthy.

The same must apply to people working in any organization. If the manager is present everywhere, and has eyes on everyone, then all can be diminished. Each feels powerless, just a small cog in a big machine. The result: each person loses identity, feels insecure, and underperforms. The manager who stands back, but is available, ready to encourage, sympathize and acknowledge, will give everyone a feeling of being appreciated. Loyalty and trust will grow.

Brother Eleutherius has been sacristan in the monastery for 45 years; he has been both conscientious and imaginative. New vestments have been bought, old ones repaired and some taken out of use. He has kept the church clean and looked after all the church vessels with great care. Brother Eleutherius is an active 63-year-old, but the new Abbot thinks there needs to be a change in the sacristy. Sadly, 45 years' dedicated work in the sacristy has not prepared him for alternative tasks in the monastery, and Brother Eleutherius fears that he will have nothing to do for the rest of his days. He is a man of great prayer, but he is also very practical and needs to keep active. The Abbot knows this and has invited him to make suggestions. But Brother Eleutherius, afflicted now with increasing deafness, fears there is nothing he can do, and his age counts against him.

How would you help Brother Eleutherius find a new way of making a positive contribution to the community?

2

People and People

Anthony Marett-Crosby
Kit Dollard

Perhaps one of the most significant similarities between the Rule and business management is the perception that all people cannot be treated the same.

Today it is accepted as good business practice that successful management of people, and businesses, begins and ends with treating every person, each employee, as an individual. This has not always been accepted as the norm – and indeed many companies only pay lip-service to the rhetoric. The change happened when the personnel function in businesses moved away from being more than administrating who was on the payroll, and began to embrace the whole issue of putting people at the forefront of management. The historians will probably relate that the Investors in People Standard[1] was more responsible than any other single instrument for achieving this. Now business management begins with recognizing and appreciating the differences in people.

The rise of the importance of Human Resources (HR)

Accepting that every person is an individual is harder than it appears. However, the business world has come a long way in the last twenty years. The rise in power and influence of the personnel department has come as a surprise to many managers. Not all of this trend has been driven by legislation or regulation. Today, it is common practice for even Small Medium Enterprises (SMEs) to have HR departments which oversee a wide range of practices including:

- Recruitment, assessment and employment of individuals.
- Continuing assessment, usually by annual performance appraisals.
- Induction, retirement and continued professional development (CPD) programmes.
- Specialist skills training at all levels.
- Mentoring and coaching programmes.
- Job description and evaluation.
- Understanding employment law, including equal opportunities rights.
- Redundancy and termination issues.
- Handling company welfare provisions, including counselling of staff.

Notice that this list does not include anything to do with the remuneration of employees!

Demonstrating the value of HR

It might be said that HR has come of age, and that its value in the workplace has now come to be recognized. One way of demonstrating this is the very significant contribution good HR practices can make to the 'bottom line' – in this case the turnover ratio of staff.

For years, companies have been handicapped in making real progress towards corporate goals by the high turnover of staff. This was particularly true of professional service firms (e.g. accountants, solicitors and chartered surveyors) who spent time and money attracting, recruiting and then training large numbers of graduates, only to find that as soon their prodigies had qualified, they moved on to another firm – or worse, left the profession – or started up their own firm of competitors. Over a two-year period it can cost £30,000 to train a chartered surveyor. In a large practice, multiply this figure by 20 for the number of entrants a year and it is obvious that a considerable sum is disappearing every time the staff 'further their careers'.

De Vere Hotels is an operating subsidiary company of Greenalls plc, which was established in 1762. The hotels are mainly good-quality four- and five-star establishments, and the company is the largest operator of five-star hotels outside London. Typical hotels are The Grand, Brighton; Mottram Hall in Cheshire; The Belfry, near Birmingham. There are 22 hotels in England and the Channel Islands. Almost 3,000 people are employed on a permanent basis. In 1992, the Board of Directors decided to work towards gaining the Investors In People award. Since then, staff throughout the company have derived many benefits. Pro-ductivity gains have funded salary increases in excess of inflation, without an overall increase in wage costs. There are extensive opportunities for career development. All job vacancies are advertised internally two weeks before any external advertising, and more than 90 per cent of key appointments are filled internally. Cumulative annual labour turnover is currently at 36 per cent, which is well below the industry average. Multiskilling, supported by qualifications, is continuous, with increased movement of staff between departments.

In other words, a significant contribution to the bottom line! In his own way, Benedict would have applauded and agreed with the sentiments behind these achievements.

But the pressure remains on the employer

Today's workforce is no longer prepared to commit to long-term company loyalty. It is no longer enough for organizations to offer financial incentives to secure the right staff. Other factors such as training, flexible working hours, family-friendly policies and company culture are becoming more important to potential workers. A reflection of this can be found in a recruitment website called newmonday.co.uk which provides search, register and advice for individuals. The website lists eight criteria for potential employees to put to employers. The first three are:

1. Establish whether a prospective employer has retention policy in place. If not, why not?
2. Establish what is most important to you, be it a clear career and development plan, a flexible contract or a manageable workload. Do not be afraid to ask about a wider benefits package.
3. Try to negotiate a training package that addresses your own skills shortfall.

The four kinds of monks

Monks do not use the phrase 'human resources', but much of what Kit has explored above from the perspective of business makes sense in the very different context of Benedict and his vision of what a monastery is about. Monks like to make themselves appear monochrome, and anyone who has visited a monastery tends to notice straight away that we do not go in for power dressing, bright colours, or any visible difference between us at all. But right at the heart of the Rule is Benedict's insistence that monks are individuals. It is not just that they are *allowed* to be different – that would be too negative – but that they are *called* to be different, and that in that diversity of character lies the real strength of the monastery, its most priceless resource.

So it is no surprise to find that Benedict opens his Rule with a discussion of the kinds of monks. He says that:

> We can all recognise the distinction between the four different kinds of monks. (RB 1)

and he goes on to give a brief but penetrating pen-portrait of each one of the four. He gives them strange names: cenobite, anchorite, sarabaite and gyrovague. We should not be put off by this. These are real people that Benedict is describing, and each one of them can be found within any monastery. More importantly, there is part of each one of these inside all of us, and that takes us close to the heart of what Benedict is trying to say.

Why are they necessarily real individuals that Benedict is describing? Might they not be the sort of cardboard cut-out figures that we sometimes use when describing characters or personalities that we want to destroy? The answer to that lies in the way that the list of the four kinds of monks came into being. It was not the result of some arid academic speculation, but as a series of descriptions written very early in monastic history out of real experience and communities. At times, these descriptions drifted towards exaggeration, as for example in the writing of Saint Jerome, who speaks of a variety of monk for whom:

> Everything is done for effect – they wear loose sleeves, flapping boots and clumsy clothing. They sigh a great deal, pay visits to virgins, criticise the clergy and eat themselves sick on every feast day. (Letter 22)

Benedict, as we have seen before, is the heir to this tradition, but also does a good job of simplifying it. The descriptions of the characters are reduced to their bare essentials. Let us see what kinds of people he is describing.

The strongest kind

The first kind of monk is apparently dismissed in a single sentence. All he says about the cenobite is that they are:

> Those who belong to a monastery where they serve under a Rule and an Abbot. (RB 1)

But if we unpack this sentence for a moment, it becomes clear that this is the kind of monk that Benedict will spend the rest of the Rule discussing. At this stage, he simply points to one key element in the identity of the cenobite which makes him 'the strongest kind'. That key is stability, the fact that the monks are part of a defined unit, pursuing a recognizable path with others. It is this grounding of the cenobite in a place, and above all in a community, that sets him apart. He is the one who knows where he is standing, where he is going and where to look for how to get there. The Rule and the Abbot provide the means for the cenobite, while the monastery provides the context for his activities.

Living alone

Benedict devotes much more space to the second kind of monk, the anchorite or hermit. For most of the early writers on monasticism, the life of the hermit was the best way to God. So Benedict is being radical when he calls the cenobite the strongest kind and puts the hermit in second place. Indeed, he argues that the hermit can only enter on his lonely way of life having:

Learnt well, from everyday experience and with the
support of many others in a community . . . They are
trained in the ranks of the brethren before they have
the confidence to do without that support. (RB 1)

So for Benedict, the life of the hermit is an option only to be
pursued after proper training – God should only be sought
alone by someone who has learned to see him first among
others. Benedict has in mind here the kind of person who
might run off to the lonely life at the first difficulty, or when the
first enthusiasm wears off. Later in the Rule, Benedict talks
about this enthusiasm when he discusses the welcoming of
new members to the community, and that kind of energy is certainly not to be despised. It just does not last. At that moment
when reality kicks in, Benedict does not want the option of the
hermit's way of life to be anything other than a dream.

What he wants, of course, is for all his monks to be long-
term players, rather than people who chop and change when
the first problems arise. He has plenty of space in his vision
of monasticism for someone who wants to seek God alone, but
that choice must be made with those around him, and not
despite or even because of them.

Their law is what they want to do
If Benedict shows himself cautious regarding the vocation of
the hermit, he abandons all moderation in his description of
a third character type, which the monastic tradition has
called the sarabaite. The description is simple but damning:

Those who have been through no period of trial under
a rule supported by the experienced guidance of a
teacher . . . go around in twos or threes or even singu-
larly, resting in sheepfolds which are not those of the
Lord but which they make to suit themselves. Their
law is what they want to do. (RB 1)

The point is pretty obvious. The sarabaite is the opposite in every important respect to the cenobite, the type of monk with which Benedict is most concerned. Where he is supported by an Abbot and by a Rule, the sarabaite invents his own rules, and allows himself the freedom to change the rules as and when he wants.

This might suggest that Benedict has no room for the innovator, for somebody able to think outside the structure. This is not the point at all, for Benedict provides a place where people can think the unthinkable, and offers a mechanism for how communities might move on, which we will explore in a later chapter. The point that Benedict has to make time and again, however, is that the engine of change is not selfish ambition but something altogether more reliable – the ambition to build up the community. Perhaps this becomes clearer when we add to Benedict's description of the sarabaite a point included in an earlier rule, which describes one of their characteristics as a tendency to:

> Think that the desert is a place of repose. (*Rule of the Master* 1)[2]

It is possible to find the equivalent of sarabaites in the business community. In the submissive role they might be the ones who are always dissatisfied, the deeply cynical, the 'murmurers'. In the aggressive role they might be the bullies – those who constantly go behind the backs of others, the arrogant.

Always on the move

The final type of monk that Benedict considers is not really a monk at all. The gyrovague is the archetypal wanderer, who uses monasticism as a cover for radical instability and lack of commitment. He is one who can never settle down, and for whom physical instability is a sign of something deeper, an inconsequential wandering away from the task in hand, and away from the memory of what we are called to do.

Here, Benedict is content to merely infer one of the most entertaining passages in the whole history of early monasticism, the description of the gyrovague in the *Rule of the Master*. This text describes the arrival of the gyrovague at a monastery, his enthusiasm for everything that he sees, and then the beginning of complaints. First of all, they are about small things and then about others more important. Finally, the gyrovague tells his community of his deep sorrow at the necessity of moving elsewhere, and the community wish him a fond farewell. So he moves on to new place, where he begins his life by rubbishing everything that he had experienced in his previous community, and saying how glad he is to have found his true home. The pattern then repeats itself as the gyrovague continues his endless round of beginnings without any focus on the goal.

Many who work in the recruitment world will recognize the character above. Of course there is a balance in obtaining an overall education in businesses before settling on a career, but too many jobs on the CV soon have future employees asking 'Just why *did* you leave Amalgamated Software Inc?' and perhaps a few inquisitive telephone calls will unearth some gyrovague characteristics! In the case of Charles, judge for yourself if he is a gyrovague.

Charles is 26 and has a degree in psychology and business studies. He has set himself the task of a high-flying career in business with the belief that it is only through the creation of wealth that he can influence others and the world for the better, and he regards this as a vocation. 'At the moment I am just finishing my sixth job in four years. Next time I will stay with the same company for several years. Some people may see this as a disadvantage, but I believe I have increased my employability. I have now worked in three different industries and made some lifelong friends. I know the inside track of the software, financial services and video cable world and have tried to learn everything they can teach me. I am now ready for the big one.'

From four to two

If these four descriptions of kinds of monks rings true for you, then you will immediately understand Benedict's more basic distinction between just two kinds of people. He does not distinguish between successes and failures, or between the leaders and the led, but something much more radical. He tells the Abbot that he:

> Must manage everything . . . so that the strong may have ideals to inspire them and the weak may not be frightened. (RB 63)

It is the realization that a monastery contains both the strong and the weak – or that there is part of both in all of us – that makes it possible for a monastery to work at all. Benedict's structure is an attempt to enable what is the strongest in us to flourish, and what is weakest in us to be allowed to change. There is something of the sarabaite and the gyrovague in us all, and Benedict knows this.

Personal qualities to be strived for

There is a variety of qualities that Benedict inspires us to reach out for. Here are six that can help in the 'daily grind' of work.

1. A call to wake up

In the Prologue and Chapter 4 Benedict gives guidelines for Christian practice – the tools of good works or qualities to be strived for. They summarize the principles of a good Christian life, but might well be applied to business life. The overall theme is about being fully human and fully alive. It is a call to wake up and join life, and it starts with a challenge at the beginning of the Prologue:

> Who is there with a love of true life and a longing for days of real fulfilment? (Pro. 15)

Well, quite frankly we all do! There is a Hungarian saying that describes how precarious life can be – 'Life is like eating honey from a thorn.' We all need more optimism and less pessimism, and it is a paradox that the 'freedom' provided by the Rule allows us to yearn for precisely this – for life in all its forms. The challenge from Benedict is about aiming high. It used to be called Positive Mental Attitude or PMA, and many companies still use the philosophy in their sales training. 'When you reach for the stars, you may not quite get them, but you won't come up with a handful of mud, either'[3] was the 'credo' of an advertising company.

We are told by Benedict that 'now is the time for us to rise from sleep'. So, first, we have to wake up, and that is not always easy – especially when we are tired of our jobs or bored or lonely. We need some inspiration – a compass to show us the way. 'Wake up . . . let us open our eyes to the light that comes from God and our ears to the voice from heaven that calls out every day.' The problem is that many of us are not sure where to turn for that vision. Benedict provides us with this 'inner compass' and is quite adamant that it will be found in two places – in God and in the community.

2. *Encouraging a sense of wonder*

In our busy world we are constantly under pressure to achieve, to perform and to produce tangible results. Very seldom do we have time to stand and stare at the wonders of the world. 'To be quite honest,' said a friend, 'the rarest bird in the world could be sitting in my garden one morning and I wouldn't know!' Benedict advises us that we should:

> cherish at all times the sense of awe with which we should turn to God. (RB 7.10)

We need to open our eyes and see God reflected in nature and in relationships with each other. Benedict encourages us to be curious, to have a sense of wonder. In other words, for those familiar with Belbin team-types, TMS or MTR-i, we are called to be Resource Investigators, Innovators and Explorers. We are encouraged to look beyond the pavements at our feet, and lift our eyes to the miracles of life around us.

Just as Benedict sees in each novice who crosses the threshold an opportunity for the community to encounter the Lord anew, so each meeting with another person is an opportunity to meet God again. It is not simply as an experience to be survived or an excuse to rush on to the next task, but to explore the uniqueness of that person.

3. *Good zeal*

Good zeal, or good spirit, can be summarized as:

> By following this path they should try to be first to show respect to one another with the greatest patience in tolerating weaknesses of body or character. (RB 72.4)

Good zeal is about the approach we bring to each day. It is more than the 'Is the glass half empty or half full?' philoso-

phy. It is 'Is the *other person's* glass half empty or half full?' It
is about goodness as a way of relating so that it becomes an
attitude, a habit. It has very little to do with competences or
how successful the other person is at doing their job. Certainly it takes trust or self-esteem, but that is true of
anything that needs attitude.

William is the Managing Director of the top firm of independent removals specialists. Many consider he is a lucky
man as he was brought into the company above all the
favourites for the job. 'I used to work for our biggest rivals.
The only reason I got this job was curiosity. I noticed that
the owner of the house in the next village was having some
major repair work done. On my way back from work, I
stopped off at the shop next to the house and asked what
was happening. "Oh," said the builders, "we are just doing
some refurbishment for the owner who lives abroad and is
thinking of selling." To cut a long story short, I met the
owner, found him a good estate agent, did the removals with
my firm and then discovered that the owner was the
chairman of this firm. He offered me a job the next week.'

Benedict would have called this good zeal. It is the process
of giving more than taking (or having attitude or faith) and
sometimes it takes a lifetime before we recognize that, in this
giving, we are receiving more than we give.

4. Building trust and respect
One of the most compelling qualities that Benedict asks us to
strive for is trust in, and respect for, others. We are asked to
create trust in those around us – it illuminates the future,
encourages obedience and gives freedom. The whole of the
Rule is about relationships, and the core quality of building

and maintaining relationships is trust. It is easier if you are living in a community of like-minded monks to do this, but it needs dedication and planning if you are living as a family or with friends: It needs an 'outside focus'. That is why we are asked to:

Place your hope in God alone. (RB 4.41)

Trust is all about teamwork and delegation, and we will look at this again under these subjects.

5. *Forgiveness*

In all human lives, things go wrong every day. Life can sometimes be a constant battle against unseen forces. 'Everything's difficult, nothing's impossible' is the motto of a nearby garage. The reality is that in living life we hurt each other, sometimes deliberately, sometimes accidentally. We need forgiveness, without which the pain or anger festers and we become dis-abled. The 'Our Father' is a wonderful resource for reconciliation:

If you have a dispute with someone, make peace with him before the sun goes down.

A hard concept to strive for in the business world, but when followed it provides peace and contentment. How to achieve this is a subject for the chapters on Making It Work and Hard Choices.

6. *Carpe Diem*

Benedict urges us to be proactive. In other words, it is no use simply being awake and hoping for opportunity to arrive on our doorstep: we have go out and make it happen. Live for each day.

Run while you have the light of life, that darkness may not overtake you. (Pro. 11)

And again:

Keep the reality of death always before your eyes, have a care about how you act every hour of your life . . . God is present everywhere. (RB 4.44)

There is a need here to be enthusiastic, to be full of life. There used to be a T-shirt which read 'LIFE, BE IN IT': surely Benedict would have worn that!

Vocations versus jobs. Does it matter?

We want to finish this chapter with a look at the whole area of vocation because it is an area where Benedict has something to say. Work dominates many lives and, because we spend so long at work, it helps if we enjoy it as well as giving our lives a sense of purpose. So when, if ever, does a job become a vocation? Can we talk about the post-room boy having a vocation? Where does a job end and a vocation begin?

There is the story of the chicken and the pig who agreed to meet for a celebratory breakfast.

'I will bring the eggs and you bring the bacon,' said the chicken. The pig looked very glum.

'What's the matter?' asked the chicken. 'It's all right for you, you are giving a contribution, I am giving total commitment!' said the pig. Sometimes the difference between vocations and jobs appears rather like this. It might help if we try to define some of the differences.

'I am giving total commitment!' said the pig.

Some characteristics of vocations and jobs

Vocation	Job
'We are called'.	We probably just fell into it.
It's poorly paid.	The market controls the going rate.
Probably not transportable.	Career portfolios.
You give everything.	Its just a 'job'.
Total job satisfaction = fulfilment.	Will live life to the full in retirement.
Inflexibility to change.	Change to survive.

Perhaps the key is matching natural gifts to jobs. Some people just fall into a career in a particular industry and when they have not quite met their aspirations (typically aged 45–55) a high level of dissatisfaction sets in. (If this happens in vocations the result is usually a higher level of burnout.) At this stage some people can adapt, change or switch jobs, and this is one of the benefits of good HR practice. Benedict would have agreed with this and made sure that the right peg was in the right hole.

In the Rule, it is assumed that everybody has a vocation and that is why the testing period is so long, but surely it would it help our businesses if all those employed felt they had a vocation? These are words from the Chairman of Mitsubishi Industries in 1998:

After careful consideration, the Board has decided that in future we will put more emphasis on employment than profit. The social effect of what we do must be the primary consideration. We will not, I repeat, *not* give our shareholders preference. If we were an American company, we would come under intense criticism for saying these things. If poor stock has no appeal for investors they can sell it straight away. Our employees have no freedom of choice and it is primarily for them that we exist.

A bold statement from a leader who shows a commitment to employees and confidence in a workforce that is stable, dedicated and going to give everything to their jobs – in other words, their vocations.

As we have seen, Benedict's people include the full variety of human strengths and weaknesses, but they need to be led in their relationships and in their work. Variety of people without leadership is chaos. The task of Benedict's leaders is to turn chaos into opportunity.

3

The Abbot Reflects . . .

One of the amazing things about a monastic community is the diversity of personalities found within it: the larger the community, the greater the spread. People don't join monasteries because they like the monk they met in the guesthouse, nor do they join simply because they find the Abbot a sympathetic character. People are attracted to the monastic life because the overall aim of that life is inherently attractive: it is answering a need deep inside their hearts. Or, as we said earlier, they have fallen in love with the God who touches them. Each monastery will deliver the dream in different ways and, as in all forms of human life, this can be both fulfilling and frustrating.

Many find community living much harder than it used to be. The strands of discontent which run through every human community, outside the monastery as well as within it, arise from a sense of exploitation, unfairness and, I fear, self-delusion. This is not new: something similar operated in Benedict's time. As Anthony has shown, many people dreamt about the monastic life and the ideal way of living it. Anthony has presented Benedict's four types – we could certainly expand and refine that number today.

Kit encourages in us a sense of wonder: does our life have to be like this? Can we make changes to improve its quality?

Certainly we know that if we want to change, we have to take the initiative. Here is some wise advice:

> If you listen with the ear and the heart you will be able to know what the other is telling you and also what he or she feels. Listen to the one who is speaking.

Creating a culture of listening is more difficult than it might appear at first sight; it is not just a question of spending time with people, although that is part of it; it is being able to perceive what goes on behind the words; to sense the feelings which give rise to the words, to realize the strength of the emotions which give power to the words.

I expect most Abbots have heard their brethren saying on one occasion or another: 'Father Abbot, you are not really listening to me!' Being able to assure someone you have listened, then to decide to do the opposite, and finally to know that the monk in question accepts the decision, is indeed a truly wonderful gift. Thus not only is the monk showing obedience, but the Abbot is displaying skills of fatherhood, empathy and clear-sightedness.

No Abbot can afford to give up the chance. Continual learning helps to avoid traps. But the key points are to make sure there is time for the brethren, to resist the temptation to predict what is going to be said – making wrong assumptions is particularly damaging – and to go on building confidence by helping each to grow.

The starting-point has to be to accept each of the monks as he is, not as he ought to be, or as the Abbot thinks he is, or indeed as the monk himself may think he is! We recognize the hermit, gyrovague and sarabaite in each of us, and see in this weakness something to be affirmed and something to be overcome. This is how we make progress in community living.

The biggest challenge an Abbot faces is to calm the eccentric, enabling him both to live in community while gently trying to tame the disruptive elements in his behaviour. Modern monks, better educated and more sophisticated than in Benedict's day, are more aware of their individuality, more volatile in community, but still capable of great virtue. The best eccentrics make immense contributions to community life, contributions the brethren grow to appreciate and accept.

This story may help us to focus upon what help the brilliant person among us may need.

Sydney is 40 years old and is the technical manager of a small computer consultancy business. The business has changed dramatically over the last twenty years as the rapid changes in the computer world have demanded. Sydney has been at the centre of these changes. His extraordinary ability enabled him to be one step ahead of the industry. As a result, his company has outflanked its competitors and now holds a key place in its town.

The company's clients include local government, the health authority and other leading businesses in the region, as well as many smaller enterprises. But Sydney has been careful to control expansion so that it can cope with demand in the area without spreading beyond it. It is enough to be the leading light in the area, and at the forefront of technical change.

Sydney has been able to identify, in this fast-changing industry, the good from the mediocre. In consequence the company has not been trapped into any deal which required it to backtrack and make a change, either in hardware or software.

Two years ago the Chief Executive, Sydney's great supporter and guru for eighteen years, retired and a new person was brought in. She was highly trained, with experience as deputy to the Managing Director in large companies. Sydney took an instant dislike to her. The chemistry between the two did not work. There was no obvious reason why this should have been so: it was just one of those things. Inevitably both, being professional, tried hard to make it work. Both felt the pressure, but Sydney rather more.

In consequence he lost heart, and the quality of his work started to suffer; the juniors working under him realized he had lost his sparkle, his inventiveness was blunted and, more distressingly, he became depressed. Joy had gone from his work. Others started to realize this.

Just at this moment, the Chief Executive was going through the books and spotted one or two things which roused suspicion: enough to take note, not enough to take further. At the heart of this suspicion was Sydney. She decided not to do anything for the moment but wait.

Over the next three months, things did not improve, though business was still brisk and customer loyalty was unaffected. At the end of that quarter the Chief Executive again noted one or two things in the books, again enough to heighten suspicion, but not enough to provide a basis for action. The pattern was repeated at the end of the next quarter as well.

At this moment the Chief Executive decided to challenge Sydney about the discrepancies. She gathered her material and called him to her office. He was not pleased at the summons, especially as it came after a particularly difficult day with one of their most loyal clients. After a minimum of pleasantries she stated her problem and presented the facts. Sydney sat looking at her dispassionately. He then said quite simply: 'If you don't trust, me I'll resign and go and find another job.' She ignored his remark and returned to the issue in hand. He remained silent; after a few seconds he got up from the desk and walked out, without a word.

What should the Chief Executive now do ?

First, we might note that during all these years Sydney has worked hard in his company because he enjoyed it and was stimulated by it. He worked because he loved what he was doing, seeing it as a 'vocation'. He was well paid, but never counted the time he spent, nor the personal sacrifices he made to ensure success. Sydney saw himself as a computer expert; it dominated his heart and mind.

The arrival of the new Chief Executive caused a shock; the old certainties were suddenly removed, he sensed he was just one of the team and he found enjoyment had gone from his work. In addition, he felt he was not being trusted. This forced to him to reflect that, after all, he was only doing a 'job', like everyone else. He realized he could drive a hard bargain to get what he wanted. His love for the company, its people and its work had been damaged. Could it be repaired?

The first duty of the new Chief Executive is to make sure she understands Sydney. Her first steps have opened up a gap. She has to try and close it. It is not just making him feel special, encouraging him, assuring him of her trust: a new relationship has to be built. It might 'cost' her dearly; it will mean a change so radical that she may not be able to achieve it.

The starting-point has to be that she should stop seeing Sydney as a 'problem' to which she can find a 'solution'. Sydney is at a crisis in his career, he needs help to make the right decisions. He cannot go back to what he was. When someone is prepared to give as Sydney, he needs to make sure he grows as a person and becomes more effective in the business. But once the Chief Executive starts to give Sydney special treatment, others will criticize her for it. She has to be prepared to say: Sydney is unique, the company needs him. And the rest of the team has to accept it. This cannot be presumed.

Benedict encourages the Abbot to adapt himself to the needs of each of the brethren without reservation. It means knowing when to challenge and when to encourage; when to criticize and when to praise. There is an underlying point: both monk and Abbot have to make the effort, however difficult. For Benedict, the search for God is at work in both parties, and the desire to make it work is overwhelming for the sake of that search.

This story about an exceptionally gifted monk poses the problem for an Abbot: how much of an exception from the common life should he allow?

Brother Ansgar is 47 years of age and has been a monk for twelve years. Before he joined the monastery he was a professional organist of some standing. He had made several recordings and been much in demand in the capitals of Europe for recitals. A man of such outstanding musical talent was rare in a monastery, but he had found there something of that desire which had led him from the international circuit of organists to a more contemplative world. His community was indeed contemplative, the brethren only rarely left the enclosure of the monastery and then only for short periods of time. It was natural that he should become abbey organist and get used to accompanying second-rate monastic voices in their daily office, which hardly changed through the year. Only rarely was he able to show forth his musical talent, playing quietly for an hour each afternoon when the rest of the monks took their siesta. Brother Ansgar was not unhappy with this arrangement. One day Brother Ansgar received a letter from the manager of a well-known recording company. They wanted to get permission to record a collection of five CDs of his organ-playing. The abbey organ was not good enough; they had already booked an organ in a church some 500 miles from the monastery. Brother Ansgar would need to spend two months, practising and recording, away from the monastery. Brother Ansgar is attracted to the idea, but recognizes it will be an exception in the monastery. He approaches the Abbot.

You may want to read a little more of this book before attempting an answer!

What sort of boss
should I be?

4

A Vision for a Leader

Anthony Marett-Crosby

One of the reasons why the Rule of Benedict has been so important in the history of Christian communities lies in Benedict's presentation of the Abbot. It is one of the greatest Christian visions of leadership, in which Benedict focuses not only on practicalities but also upon how he wants the leader to lead. Almost every model of authority and service within the Church is drawn, either directly or indirectly, from Benedict – his perception into leadership is perhaps his greatest gift to the Christian centuries.

Abbots have very often been called upon to manage not only monks – this is difficult enough – but also large business enterprises. For about five centuries, large tracts of England were owned by monasteries, and Abbots exercised huge authority as landowners and businessmen. Some of them sat in Parliament at a time when it was a gathering of those who held land, and therefore power, in the realm. Even today, although monasteries no longer exercise this sort of role, a modern Abbot is called upon to be both Spiritual Father and Chief Executive. Yet the practicalities, the day-to-day business of making a community work, can only ever be half of the story. They depend upon Benedict's fundamental understanding of what an

Abbot is, and how an Abbot might be a leader of his community.

Benedict answers this by exploring a number of images of
authority, each of which reveals something of the dynamic of
leadership. No one image is exclusive of another, and nor
should any image have priority. It is in their interaction that
Benedict sees their power, not only to achieve ends, but to
inspire the variety of characters which, as we now know, find
themselves in a monastery.

The name itself

What exactly is an Abbot? If we want to understand that, we
have to start by exploring the name itself, which has a history
so long and complicated that Benedict feels a need to summarize it. This is what he says.

> Anyone who aspires as Abbot or Abbess to be
> superior of a monastery should always remember
> what is meant by the title . . . It is the place of
> Christ that the superior is understood to hold in the
> monastery by having a name which belongs to
> Christ. (RB 2)

This is pretty serious stuff, because what it says is that the
name Abbot points to something far above any normal
model of authority. It points to God himself, for Benedict
wants his Abbot to be 'another Christ', to hold the same
place in a monastery that Christ does in the heart of a
believer. It invites the Abbot to be an imitator of Christ, as
the one who held authority and offered, in his own life, an
image of how to be of service to others. All the images that
Benedict uses come from this basic conception of authority
as a way of following Christ first of all, and then of being
like Christ to others.

This double calling of the Abbot was not actually invented by Benedict. It goes back to the earliest men and women who lived the monastic life in the Egyptian desert, among whom certain individuals were marked out as *Abbas* (spiritual fathers) or *Ammas* (spiritual mothers). Their authority was enormous, because of the obedience that they inspired in their disciples.

So there is a story told of an Abba who commanded his disciple to plant a piece of dry wood in the desert and to water it every day. The disciple had to bring the water from a long way off, but he did it every day for three years, out of obedience to his Abba. At the end of this time, the dry stick bore fruit, and the disciple became in his turn a great monastic teacher, known to us as John the Short.

You might long for the sort of respect that can enable people to water dry sticks – alternatively, you may find the story absurd. But consider the reason it was told, not to encourage the planting of sticks but to be an image of the power of the Abba as one whose closeness to God could inspire others. It was said of another early monk, that:

When the men of the word saw a man of God in their midst, they were eager to become Christians and faithful.

The Abba is meant to inspire this eager desire, what Benedict calls zeal in the Rule. Benedict's Abbot is the sign of Christ, the sign of hope, for his monks.

Let us pause for a moment here, and ask what signs Benedict gives a community by which they can recognize the Abbot as another Christ. If this question sounds a bit remote for you, ask it this way – what sign can you give that you are exercising leadership for anyone other than yourself? Benedict suggests something very important in response to this when he commands his Abbot to lead his community by 'a two-fold teaching'.

In the first place, this refers to the words the Abbot uses, the orders he gives and the inspiration he provides by his teaching. Obviously this is important, but we all know how little words can actually mean when they are uttered by someone who doesn't actually live them, which is why Benedict, ever the realist, tells Abbots that:

> The example of the lives they lead . . . is the most important way . . . they use in their teaching. (RB 2)

That is how Benedict wants his Abbot to be recognized for what he is, somebody who leads for the sake of service. The sign of that lies in the way the Abbot himself lives.

One of the first monks to lead a community of others was Pachomius, who lived in Egypt in the fourth century. His first community came together in an abandoned village on the edge of the River Nile, and it was an experiment in how to lead a group. There is no record at all that he ever said anything very much to them – in a sense he could not, as there was no theory or experience on which he could draw. He was a pioneer, so he could only teach in one way, which was by how he himself lived. Thus it is recorded in an ancient life of Pachomius that 'he became their servant', and this was the model of leadership that he adopted. His hope was that this model of service would do two things. In the first place, he was struggling to find a way in which people could actually live together. He recognized that an integral part of leadership lay in providing for common needs, and to this extent it worked well. But his second hope was to be frustrated. He wanted those around him to see this model of service not only as a way of getting things done, but as something that might inspire them to take on the same kind of way of life. This they never did. So powerful was his model of service that they started to treat him with contempt, as a slave. Pachomius' reaction was to try more and more to make them see what he was doing, although in the end things got so bad that he had to chase them out of the monastery and start again. He learned that he needed to explain what he was doing, as well as do it, although the model of leadership by service was something he never abandoned.

When monasteries have gone wrong in history, it has very rarely been because of an inadequacy at the level of theory: it has been when those called to leadership have failed to be living signs of anything beyond themselves. I wonder, is the same true of business?

This twofold teaching, by life as much as by word, carries with it an important consequence. To be a sign, and to speak the right words, the Abbot must be able to listen and willing to learn from what he says.

> After hearing the advice of the community, the superior should consider it carefully in private and only then make a judgment. (RB 3)

Benedict emphasizes that the leader is on the same path towards God as everyone else, that he is as much pupil in the school of the Lord's service as he is a teacher. Benedict expresses this starkly in his chapter on the election of Abbot:

They should always bear their own frailty in mind.
(RB 64.18)

The Shepherd

The first image that Benedict uses of his Abbots follows on
directly from the Christ-centred language we have been
exploring. He portrays the Abbot as a shepherd, and not just
any ordinary shepherd.

> They should follow the living example of the Good
> Shepherd who left 99 of his flock on the mountains
> and went off to look for the one sheep who had
> strayed. So great was his compassion for the weakness
> of that one erring sheep that he actually lifted it onto
> his sacred shoulders and so carried it back to the rest
> of the flock. (RB 27)

I want you to think about that image for a minute – a manager
who leaves 99 per cent of his assets at risk to go in search of
the 1 per cent which, because of its own weakness, has gone
astray. Looked at in this way, the story is evidently stupid, a
quite unrealistic way of managing anything. So is this what
Benedict wants? Let us look at some of the ways in which
Benedict explores this image of shepherd in the Rule.

In the first place, Benedict's shepherd is undoubtedly a
leader. While there are certainly proper roles for various subordinate officials in the monastery, Benedict wants his
readers to be in no doubt about the chain of command, about
where the buck stops:

> It is best, in the interests of preserving peace and
> charity, that the authority for the whole administra-
> tion of the monastery should rest with the Abbot.
> (RB 65)

. . . carried it back to the rest of the flock.

To the shepherd, then, is undoubtedly entrusted this task of
leadership, but it is leadership with a difference. The story of
the shepherd who leaves his flock in search of the one who
has strayed is a key to the kind of leadership Benedict wants
him to exercise, since it keeps in mind the basic distinction
upon which the Rule hinges: it is a responsibility for both the
strong and the weak. What Benedict wants his leader to
remember is that one sheep is different from another, and
that, as such:

> It is the task of the Abbot to adapt with understanding
> to the needs of each, so that they may not only avoid
> any loss but even have the joy of increasing the
> number of good sheep in the flock committed to them.
> (RB 2)

If you have read the quotation above in a hurry, then stop
and read it again. It contains Benedict's prescription for
how to keep the monastery afloat, not in terms of money but
something more basic, the increase in the size of the
community. The willingness of the leader to be open to differences between people is what Benedict places in the
centre – uniformity of treatment is presented as a recipe for
disaster.

Healer and doctor

This image of the shepherd as someone who leads by understanding is taken further in a second image of the leader – as
healer or doctor. If a monastery is not a club for saints, then it
might in some ways be described as a healing community, a
place where people come, discover they are not all they
should be, and then find ways of growing in their strengths
and living with their weaknesses.

It is the Abbot, the person who knows those whom he leads,

who is called upon to exercise this role, but only because he exercises it for himself first. Benedict's image of a leader is not as somebody perfect, but rather as somebody who:

> . . . knows how to heal his own wounds and those of others. (RB 46)

This is a call to honesty, not only about others – which tends to be easy – but also about the leader himself. Only with this honesty in place can the Abbot become what he is called – and can act as the wise physician with regard to the needs, difficulties and even sins of the community.

It is important to note that, in this task of healing, Benedict does not imagine that the Abbot is alone. This becomes clear in Benedict's chapter on those who refuse to change their way of life, even after the disruptive effect of their behaviour has been made clear. Benedict expects his leader to have a variety of remedies, and some of these involve others, people whom the leader knows who have skills that he perhaps has not.

> Therefore the superior should use every curative skill as a wise doctor does, for instance by sending in *senpectae,* that is mature and wise members of the community who may discreetly bring counsel to one who is in a state of uncertainty and confusion. (RB 27)

This implies, of course, that the Abbot has already identified such people, that he is prepared to share with them at least this part of the burden of his office. If that fails, then there is always another solution, namely to ask the whole community to pray for the one who is wandering. Only if that fails should the Superior take up the tools of that other kind of doctor, the surgeon:

> The superior must turn to the knife for amputation
> . . . lest one diseased sheep corrupt the whole flock.
> (RB 28)

The steward

There is not much that is terribly comforting or easy about Benedict's image of leadership. This is because he takes it seriously, as a task done not for the glorification of the leader but for the good of others. Critical in this regard is the image of the Abbot as steward, which at its most simple reminds the leader that his time of authority is limited, that he will not be there for ever. For much of the history of the Benedictine order, Abbots have held office for life, but the image of stewardship in the Rule even goes beyond the grave. Thus Benedict demands that the Abbot:

> Must often think about the demands made by the burden he has undertaken and consider to whom he will have to give an account of the stewardship. (RB 64)

Who is the person to whom the Abbot is accountable? Benedict of course is referring to the one from whom all power comes, namely God. If the Abbot as healer has a care for his own inner life, he will not want to bear the burden of failing to live up to his stewardship.

Although this points to heaven, it also functions as the beginning of the practical realism for which Benedict is famous. Images of shepherd and healer can seem more than a little idealistic, whereas the language of steward is entirely practical. At the top of Benedict's in-tray is the care of souls, and he commands the Abbot not to become too distracted by 'the fleeting and temporal things' which might crowd this out.

So the image of steward enables him to propose a necessary delegation, saying that:

> The superior should entrust the property of the monastery to various members of the community whose character and reliability inspire confidence. (RB 32.1)

There are two important points about this last quotation, both of which we will discuss later in the book. In the first place, Benedict is not saying that things like material goods don't matter. Actually, he is saying quite the reverse – the property and business of the monastery matter so much that they should be handled as something more than our own private property, to do with them whatever we will. Second, the image of steward once again requires that the Abbot knows the people around him. Time and again, we return to this.

As a result of this, stewardship takes time. Perhaps because of this, Benedict understands delegation as involving a sharing of stewardship. So he establishes the principle that:

> The monastery is a monastery of God and should always be wisely administered by those who are wise themselves. (RB 53)

Delegation will form a subject in its own right later in the book. Here, we need to note just one point about it, since this informs our understanding of the Abbot as leader. Of all the four images that Benedict uses – Christ, shepherd, healer and steward – only the last can truly be delegated. There cannot be more than one shepherd, nor multiple Christs, and the task of healing the sick is so delicate that it can only be shared in rare circumstances. Stewardship by contrast demands to be shared, precisely because it is so serious.

Writing many centuries after Benedict, but firmly within the monastic tradition, Saint Bernard told a new Pope:

> I exhort you to use every means to avert from yourself the onslaught of things that are the duties of others. Remain unaware of many things. (*De Consideratione* 4.21)[1]

5

Benedict's Leaders

Kit Dollard

This chapter is about leadership in business and how the job of a leader compares with that of the Abbot, so if you are not interested in this aspect of business or you are fed up with yet more words on the subject, then skip on.

The problem with leadership theories is that there are so many of them. When we are being led well we can recognize it (e.g. Winston Churchill in the Second World War). When we are led badly, we an also recognize it (e.g. Captain Bligh). What follows is a brief review of leading theorists and writers on leadership who can be drawn into this conversation with Benedict.

We have not made a difference between leaders and managers. In business circles there can be some debate about the difference between the two functions, but in this context we are talking about leadership.

An initial reflection on leadership with Benedict

For many people in work today, the role of leader can come at quite a 'junior' level – not only in age and experience but also in job situation. For example, the high level of responsibility of most medical and hospital jobs, including those at a 'low' level, may require a high level of leadership. In fact all jobs have a great deal of responsibility, and this is not always realized or acknowledged. If you do not believe this, look at the qualities of leadership below and ask yourself which nurse or hospital porter would you rather have look after you on your next visit to hospital? So here is a challenging question – how much leadership training do our employees get?

These days Abbots, when appointed, do not attend an Abbots' course – unlike fast-track executives, headteachers or newly appointed directors. There is not even an MBA for 'suitable' monks. So where do they get their training? The answer is in the school of the Lord's service, which is of course the monastery or the community. Perhaps we should be training our own leaders in our own organizations and communities? Certainly it would be less theoretical, with more of an industry focus, and perhaps it would serve our businesses better.

Can leadership be taught, or is it something you have to learn for yourself? What about 'born leaders'? Certainly there are key personality traits that have to be present, but leadership is the supreme example of experiential learning – experiencing, reflecting, theorizing and testing. It is in this experience that leadership becomes part of an individual's personality. We may then become what others would call 'a born leader' but it is only because we have had the opportunity to lead, reflect, adapt and implement that we attain the leadership needed for the particular job. Benedict would have recognized this, and that is why he wrote down so clearly his instructions on the gifts and behaviour of his leaders.

So what is leadership?

A definition of leadership is important if we are to have a conversation with Benedict. Field Marshal Slim said 'Leadership is a mixture of example, persuasion and compulsion . . . in fact it is just plain you.' Warren Bennis, an American writer, defines leadership as 'the capacity to create a compelling vision and sustain it'. He adds, 'with a vision, the leader provides the all-important bridge from the present to the future of the organisation.'[1]

Richard Higginson, a writer on Christian leadership, says that leaders should first and foremost be 'wise as serpents, innocent as doves'. He suggests that there are tensions in any leader between idealism which should be tempered by realism, principles by shrewdness and integrity by astuteness.

John Adair says that leaders must have leadership qualities.[2] He emphasizes that each job needs different leadership qualities. If you were to make a list of the qualities of leadership needed for your particular job, they might be different from those listed below, or they might include some similarities. Here are seven qualities that are commonly found in leaders:

1. *Integrity* – goodness, truth and the fact that others trust you.
2. *Enthusiasm* – without this, very few will even listen to you.
3. *Resilience* – needed when unpopular decisions have to be made.
4. *Fairness* – impartiality in giving rewards or penalties.
5. *Humility* – working for an arrogant leader is always difficult.
6. *Warmth* – leadership needs heart as well as mind.
7. *Confidence* – people will always sense a lack of this! So this needs to be one of the first qualities to be developed.

Leadership theories of management in conversation with Benedict

Leadership can sometimes best be seen in power, and this is a good starting-point. French and Raven[3] identified five sources of power and criteria to which leaders should aspire. These 'levers' could be used to measure success.

1. *Coercive* – the stick, being able to punish people in some way.
2. *Reward* – the carrot, being able to reward team members.
3. *Referent* – possessing a personal charisma.
4. *Legitimate* – having the necessary 'mandate' to do the job.
5. *Expertise* – having the competence and experience to do the job.

At first sight, Benedict's Abbot may indeed wield significant power, but it is a power with 'awesome' responsibility, for

> they should remember that they will have to account in the awesome judgment of God both for their own teaching and also for the obedience of their disciples. (RB 2.6)

Imagine a company Chairman being given that level of responsibility!

Other early leadership theories started by having a fairly functional approach to the job. Theorists such as Fayol, Koontz and O'Donnell put leadership styles on a continuum from Democratic to Autocratic:

Democratic  Autocratic

Initially, it is tempting to think that there are indeed two ways to lead, and you might quote RB 2.25 for instructions to

Abbots to 'use the encouragement of a loving parent and now the threats of a harsh disciplinarian'. However, Benedict needs his leaders to go further than this, so he introduced that instruction with 'Thus in adapting to changing circumstances . . .' It is this that allows us a clue as to what he really wants of his leaders.

Mintzberg suggested that organizations are divided into seven types and that managers are involved in a range of activities broken into three areas – interpersonal, informational and decision-making roles. Here we have the small beginnings of treating individuals and organizations as different, and we can see glimpses of something in common with Benedict.

Charles Handy, a British writer and broadcaster who was Warden of St George's House in Windsor (a centre for business ethics), took a Christian approach and focused on management by mistakes – among other issues. He believed that managers should learn to forgive mistakes and not always punish, because that is how learning takes place. Handy believed in federal organizations which needed subsidiarity (which had to be built on trust and confidence) and employees who looked for opportunities to push the boundaries of their jobs. Again, there is a maturity here that is very Bendictine.

Like Mintzberg, there are similarities with Benedict here in practice. It might be summed up in the philosophy of 'managing everything in the monastery so that the strong may have ideals to inspire them and the weak not be frightened away by excessive demands'.

Peter Senge is a systems theorist who argues that, for businesses to survive in today's world, they have to be able to cope with continuous change. They have to become 'learning organisations'. Any monastery that fails to become a learning organization will soon fade away. That is why the title of the final chapter of the Rule is called 'only a beginning' and includes:

We however blush with shame when we reflect on the
negligence and inadequacy of the lives we live.
(RB 73.7)

This is an admission of our failures and a commitment to
improve.

Monasteries are in it for the long term. Certainly they are
helped by the 'stability of the workforce' but more important
is the strategic aim or mission. The idea of building a number
of systems, like Senge, to achieve that strategy would not
have been so foreign to Benedict. Of course, it needs to be
combined with a commitment to developing people, but that
is already present in the Rule.

Rensis Likert, an American social psychologist, conducted
significant research into human behaviour. He distinguished
four systems of management that favoured the final system
(System 4) as it produced higher productivity, greater involve-
ment of individuals and better management relations.
According to Likert, management is always a relative process,
with leaders needing to adapt their behaviour to take account
of the people they lead. Perhaps here we see an example of
management theory 'catching up' with St Benedict.

Difference strokes for different folks

Hersey and Blanchard were perhaps the first to widely
propose a more flexible model to leading others, and in their
case it was based on the experience and competence of the
follower.[4] They defined a difference between a task-centred
approach and a relationship-centred approach to leadership.
Task behaviour was 'the extent a leader defines the duties
and responsibilities of an individual or group'. Leaders tell
people what to do, how to do it, when to do it, where to do it
and who is to do it. Relationship behaviour is 'the extent a
leader engages in a two-way communication'. This means lis-

tening, encouraging, facilitating and providing clarification.

Hersey and Blanchard suggested that the communication style used should reflect the maturity of the subordinate being led – balancing relationship with the subordinate and the task needing to be completed. They suggested four possible styles:

1. *Telling* – Low relationship, high task.
2. *Selling* – High relationship, high task.
3. *Participating* – High relationship, low task.
4. *Delegating* – Low relationship, low task.

The great advantage of this theory is that it provides a pattern for leading teams, which have different levels of ability, commitment and maturity. In other words 'different strokes for different folks'.

Benedict would probably have shied away from anything so formal or rigid as the model above, but he would have endorsed its philosophy. His images of the Abbot point to the variety of personalities in the community and therefore the need to lead followers with appropriate styles. It also provides an excellent framework for delegation. Delegation is really about entrusting authority and power to others. The reality is that, however good we are at our jobs, we will have to get others involved if we are going to complete the tasks that we – or our teams – are hoping to achieve.

Balancing the different needs of the team

John Adair has made his reputation by using many of the Army's methods in his teachings. His 'action-centred' leadership focuses on three main concerns for the leader – the task, the individual and the team. As the task develops in different circumstances, the leader needs to concentrate on one area more than the other. For example, if the team's deadline looked as though it was going to be missed, the leader might concentrate on a more task-orientated approach as the cost of ignoring individuals' sensitivities, personalities or creativity. On the other hand, if one of the team members looked to be in trouble, then the leader may decide to concentrate on a more person-centred approach through support and motivation, while accepting that the deadline might take second priority.

Adair claimed that the main functions of leadership are:

- Defining the task.
- Planning.
- Briefing.
- Controlling.
- Evaluating.
- Motivating.
- Organizing.
- Providing an example.

Adair and Benedict have a lot in common, although Benedict would probably not have expressed it in this way! The tension between the three areas of needs of the team as shown above (people, task and team or community) expresses much of what the Rule seeks to address about people living together. Benedict tries to do this through his advice to the Abbot about leadership.

The responsibility for the person:

> They should remember always that the responsibility they have taken is that of guiding souls and that they will have to render an account of the guidance they have given. (RB 2.31)

The responsibility for the task:

Let us set ourselves high standards (RB Pro 21)

and

The superior should manage everything so prudently that the saving work of grace may be accomplished in the community and whatever duties the community undertakes may be carried out without any excuse for murmuring. (RB 41)

The responsibility for the team or community:

In drawing up regulations, we hope to set down nothing harsh, nothing burdensome. The good of all concerned however may prompt us to a little strictness in order to amend faults and to safeguard love. (Pro. 46 and 47)

The importance of good example

Adair provides a further area of common ground – that of leading by example. Perhaps it is old-fashioned, but it is central to both Adair and Benedict. It is inconceivable that Benedict's Abbots should merely issue instructions without first setting the example themselves. This is a call to action – it is difficult to do much pointing from behind a computer VDU or an e-mail. There is a requirement to get out and actually do some example-setting. In other words, Benedict's leaders are leading for the sake of service. In a way, the Adair model of leadership is about service also – for training military leaders has always been about example. It is no coincidence that the motto of the Royal Military Academy, Sandhurst, is 'Serve to Lead'.

Being a leader is a responsibility and this

> inspires them (Abbots) to greater care of their own
> souls. By encouraging through their faithful ministry
> better standards for those in their care, they will
> develop higher ideals in their own lives. (RB 2.39 –40)

It is this paradox that helps make Benedict so appealing. As any speaker or business trainer will admit, there is nothing like the task of having to prepare a subject for delivery to a sceptical group of trainees to encourage thorough preparation and excellent delivery on that subject. In other words, by leading others you will improve yourself.

The equality of leadership

Benedict emphasizes that the leader is on the same path towards God as everyone else. When the Abbot has finished his spell of eight years, he is still a member of that community and has to return there. The vow of stability ensures that the community is his family, and that is where he will return. In the same way Adair's leaders are not to be considered a class apart but are also 'right in the thick of it'.

Benedict's leaders are such a good example that recruitment should not be a problem, as the leader's example will 'increase the number of good sheep committed to them'. Occasionally, recruitment problems are solved by teams of like-minded individuals networking for projects. Occasionally there are duos, like the powerful Lords Hanson and White, but how often do employees join a company because of the example of the leader? Is there not an area for improvement here? Just how often do leaders get involved in the recruitment process?

Striving for balance

Stephen Covey is an international writer and consultant on management theories. His best-known book *The Seven Habits of Highly Effective People*[5] is a best-seller and the principles he writes about have many similarities in our conversation with Benedict. In the chapter on 'Principles of Interpersonal Leadership', Covey highlights the benefits of the 'Win/Win' situation. To put it another way, it is the theory of Transactional Analysis – behaving like a Parent, Child or Adult (aggressive, submissive or assertive). In the Win/Win situation (Adult to Adult, or assertive behaviour) everybody benefits. Covey insists that the axes are a matter of balancing courage with consideration.

High		
	Lose/Win	Win/Win
		Consideration
	Lose/Lose	Win/Lose
Low		
	Low	High
	Courage	

Here we have an example of a Benedictine principle – striving for reasonable balance by trying to ensure a Win/Win outcome in all relationships (but there are few monastic followers who would understand it in these words!)

In trying to implement the Win/Win situation in leadership in personal relationships, Covey claims there are five elements which need to be considered – the desired results, establishing guidelines, identifying resources, accountability, and the consequences. All these elements make up the balance needed by Benedict's leaders. So finally, let us look at what some of these elements might be.

Some final words about leadership – the balance of Benedict's leaders

One of the hallmarks of Benedict's Abbots is that they should 'not impose any thing that is harsh or burdensome' (RB Pro 46). That sums up very well a philosophy of leadership that can be found not only in many modern leadership theories but also in examples of today's successful leaders. An example would be a secretary asking to leave work early to go home and change for a special date at the theatre; to which the answer from a good leader would be 'Of course' (provided of course that this was not the fifth time that week or that the team work load was suffering!).

It was clear from the chapter on Leadership by discernment that Benedict's leaders are concerned, first and foremost, with balance in life. Here are some more examples of Benedict's balance as a leader. He says that:

 . . . no one is to overwork. (RB 31.7/53.18)

 . . . there is to be a modification of food allowance. (RB 39.6)

. . . no one should be exonerated from kitchen duty except in the case of . . . (RB 35.1)

. . . we should drink in moderation and not until we are full. (RB 40)

This is all sound management practice, but, you might ask, who decides what is overwork? The fact is that Benedict treats his followers like adults who can make decisions for themselves. This is the sign of a confident leader who can treat his followers like adults. And yet, being human means there will be failings. The key qualities are trust, mutual respect and concern for those entrusted to the leader's care.

The images of the Abbot as servant, shepherd, doctor and steward signify that much has been given in terms of responsibility and power. But there is a contrast to many of today's leaders in business who have seized the power but not the responsibility. In the final reckoning, it is God who will be the judge – not shareholders, clients, suppliers or even governments. And that is true of all of us, believers or not.

6

The Abbot Reflects . . .

I wonder what you are expecting, having read those two contrasting chapters!

Some people think that being elected an Abbot is 'promotion'. Every Abbot will remember the moment his election was called and the immediate sense of inadequacy. The task is so much greater than anything else in the monastery, however large one's responsibilities.

The 'power' of the Abbot over each monk is immense, but if wrongly used he takes responsibility for all the dreadful consequences that result. The Abbot's role, as Anthony has expressed, is to be Christ among the brethren, but knowing all the time that Christ is alive in their hearts, they offer an alternative explanation, if the need arises.

The monk, like everyone else, is endowed with a healthy quota of self-interest. The inspiration to become a monk glows bright at the moment of self-giving, but it is difficult to keep it burning so brightly as time passes. Benedict provides the Abbot with the safeguard of obedience. Each member of the community has vowed obedience to the Abbot and the community; he accepts what he asks him to do for the community, and realizes that his life is dedicated to service in the community. That is the consequence of his decision to join and of his acceptance by the community.

This puts the Abbot in a position which may differ from that of Chief Executives. They may be able to hire and fire, and if necessary pay the consequences through the courts, but they have far less power over an employee's personal life. They may demand loyal obedience of their workforce, but this cannot reach beyond the gate. Each monk thinks carefully before joining a community; once they have made that commitment, they know they cannot withdraw. The responsibility on the Abbot becomes much greater.

Pondering Kit's definition of leaders and the links with Benedict, I find myself saying, 'Yes, it is all very well, but . . .' Like all theory, it may not match the realities of the moment, the daily experience, the unexpected crisis. These definitions may be important for interview panels when evaluating the merits of the candidates for a particular job.

Four pieces of advice I was given shortly after my election illustrate the priorities I have given to the tasks of the Abbot. At the same time they may offer a monastic contribution to the tasks of the business manager as outlined by Kit. The agendas may be different, but the approach to those in our care has many similarities, suggesting that the role of the Abbot in caring for his monks, and the role of the business manager to get the best out of his employees converge.

Blessed are you if you can distinguish a speck of dust from a mountain; you will avoid for yourself and others a goodly amount of vain worries.

In the hurly-burly of daily life it is so easy to over-react to some things and lose the right perspective. It is so easy to over-react to the monk who comes to one's door to apologise, when you know the relationship between you is not good. The poor man leaves thinking the world has fallen in, when all he has done is put a dent in the car. The same must be true in business: the junior manager might make a mistake which means production stops for two minutes; only five minutes before it was due to close down for the day, and the manager screams and yells at the man, as if a whole day's production has been lost.

And there are plenty of reasons why this might happen; the Superior or manager is too tired, or has got something else on his mind; the relationship with the individual concerned has been deteriorating over the last few weeks and this is the last straw, or it just happened that the factory was trying to achieve record production that week, and the loss of two minutes scuppered it.

The result – an explosion. This further ruptures the relationship, damages self-confidence and brings embarrassment to both parties. Nothing constructive has been achieved. All because they could not distinguish a speck of dust from a mountain.

This story shows how a speck of dust became a mountain.

Hector is the Managing Director of a printing business specializing in small booklets, reports and other documents. In addition they do colour printing, invitations, visiting cards, printed notepaper and similar products.

Most customers live within 50 miles of the factory. Given its long history, the company has become very much part of the town; it sponsors cultural and sporting events in the locality. It has a good reputation as a fair employer with a loyal workforce and supportive of their families. The town is supportive and justly proud of the company.

Hector was brought into post from outside. His predecessor had held the job for 25 years and was well liked and respected. After his departure the Directors wanted someone from outside, skilled in printing and in business management. His first task was to bring the business up to date. Although his predecessor had started to introduce new technology, much still needed to be done. The workforce was confused and wanted to know where they were going: they feared for their jobs.

Hector was one among many talented applicants for the job of Managing Director. His CV showed he had worked in a large printing business producing books and magazines. This business had been through the trauma of change and emerged stronger. He was familiar with the difficulties. He had the right qualifications, a good degree, post-graduate training and, after ten years, an MBA. He knew, at the age of 38, this was the challenge he had been waiting for.

After two years in post, Hector was beginning to lose his enthusiasm: he had reached an impasse. The business needed to change but the staff were reluctant, even resistant. More critically, he had failed to win over his most senior colleagues. They wanted change to come slowly, allowing each member of the team to adjust with minimum fuss. Hector thought it would take too long and would put the business under threat.

Hector was not good at dealing with people. He had spent so much time at his desk and keeping in touch with his family, who had still not moved house to be near the factory. Hector had not had a minute to get to know his staff as people with families. He does not appreciate that one employee is scared of losing his job because he is under financial pressure paying for the further education of his children. He needs his job for three years. He is reluctant to co-operate with Hector because he thinks this will make him a prime candidate for redundancy. How does he persuade his employees to change their working methods?

This is an example of how someone can become so absorbed in his job that he fails to see the wider issues – and failing to see them, he does not give them the priority they require.

The future of the business is not only dependent on strategic plans, investment in new machinery and looking for new outlets; it is also about the deeper worries of the families, of those who work there and those in the town where the business is important.

The second piece of advice: *if the organization you have set up functions well, it will also function well in your absence.* Wisdom, stemming from experience, will allow you to be a good administrator, without servile dependence on experts, without putting absolute confidence in strategic plans, and without abandoning common sense in favour of the promises of future inventions.

Every Abbot makes an act of trust in each of his brethren, and on that trust is built everything else. Whatever the work the monk is asked to do, he will know that the Abbot has considered the matter carefully before making the request. The monk may not like the task, but he will know that the Abbot will rely on his dedication to the life to give his best to the task he has asked him to do. It is in the light of that dedication that the Abbot takes responsibility if the task is not done as well as he wanted.

That sounds like a 'high-risk' strategy – indeed it is! The abbey will have diverse activities for the monks, and few of them will be specially trained. Whatever the activity, it presents a challenge to the monk, by which he grows both as human being and as monk. The work the monk does is as much part of his journey to God as being in choir saying his prayers. It is not that one takes the place of the other, but of both fitting together as part of a full day. This work may be quite secular, like fundraising for the community, or it might be apostolic, like running a parish, or it may require scholarship, like teaching in a school or university.

Whatever the task, the Abbot appoints people to posts not simply because of what they have achieved already, but also for their potential in the future. In making these appointments he will ensure that the 'organization' of the monastery will be strengthened and, at the same time, he trusts the brethren to do the jobs to the best of their ability.

In all this the Abbot listens to the brethren and responds to their suggestions and ideas, but he has to keep a true sense of balance between work, community life and prayer. The business should be large enough for the community to control, but not so big that it imposes alien values or undue burdens on the daily life of the community. In this respect the aims of the monastery and secular business diverge: different agendas are at work.

It always remains important for the Abbot to listen to the brethren, especially when they are concerned that work is dominating their life. No doubt it is equally important for managers to listen to the voice of those under them.

This story enables us to reflect on the need to listen.

Conchita is half Spanish and half English. Her family live in Spain but she has been educated in England and is fully bi-lingual; indeed, she is also fluent in French, having studied the language at university. She has a good 2:1 degree in languages, and, with her lively Latin temperament, she has been advised that she could apply for a job anywhere and succeed.

She decided to qualify as an accountant, which would give her the skills to travel the world and then settle down to a rewarding job. After qualifying she moved to a bigger, international firm of accountants. She found herself as the junior in a small team of experienced accountants, all men.

Conchita was a Catholic but would not have regarded

herself as 'committed' in the usual sense of that word. But she says her prayers and has no doubt that she ought to go to Mass more often. Beneath that she leads a sober life of high moral principles.

Her team is very busy. They have a number of prestigious clients whose annual audit is both important for the firm, but also demanding of the auditors because their businesses are complex. It offers Conchita the challenge she wants.

Soon after starting, she finds herself working late most evenings to keep to the schedule set by the senior partners. She is much engrossed in the work and challenged by it. The first year goes well and she receives good assessments. She is marked down as a young accountant with potential.

In her second year she becomes aware that her senior colleagues are trying to portray a particular picture for their client's finances. All agree the answer will not infringe the professional boundaries of honesty or legality. Conchita notes that some senior colleagues are colluding in statements which, while not inaccurate in themselves, seem to slide along the edge of honesty.

This worries Conchita, but she has no one to talk to about it. She could not speak to the senior partners: they would simply say she was reading more into this than was meant. She has not been with the company long enough to command attention. She is too junior to request a change of team, and anyway another team may be no different, so she decides to continue where she is for the moment. A year later, her anxieties have not been allayed; indeed, she has become even more suspicious.

As it happened, she went to a special meeting arranged by her local church for young professional people. She went more out of loyalty and curiosity than anything else. There she met a young theologian, researching into business ethics. Many were concerned at the huge salaries so many earned in London, especially stockbrokers, financial analysts, bankers, accountants and lawyers. How could this be justified in a world with such disparity of earnings? The discussion moved away from wage differentials towards the way companies express themselves. It was claimed that figures are manipulated to give an impression which is inaccurate. In this discussion several moral issues were examined; the difference between intention and act, the difficulty of establishing when something was right or wrong, the importance of conscience in determining one's life.

From this, Conchita became aware that the unease she felt sprang from her conscience, unformed but active. She had to read more about the values lying behind behaviour – not just in the obvious areas, but also in her professional life, and the way she prepared her reports.

But, she asks herself, should she continue to work in the team?

We have seen that at the heart of Benedict's Abbot is the ability to listen, pick up signals, and deal with them before they become a crisis. This may sometimes be absent from the qualities Kit has outlined in his description of Leadership Theories.

At the heart of listening is being awake to the voice of conscience. All superiors, whatever their expertise, must be able to listen if they are to lead effectively. They must be especially sensitive to the voice of conscience. Some consciences may be over-sensitive, others may be underdeveloped, but the point here is to give time and listen carefully to the issues.

The third piece of advice: *life grows slowly; never despair.*

Life grows slowly; never despair.

On the whole, monks change slowly. They find sudden change de-stabilizing and threatening. In this they are not different from the rest of the human race! An Abbot, especially when newly elected, can think sudden change is a good thing, but care is needed.

The Abbot relies on the goodwill of his brethren. There are always some in a community who want to move faster, but such speed may represent an ill-considered desire for change or be driven by other motives. For whatever reason, the Abbot knows he must proceed with care. Slow change also refers to that inner process we call conversion of heart; the Abbot, in whatever ways he can, inspires his brethren to continue pursuing that radical change in attitude and behaviour. It is, as we said at the beginning, part of the process of becoming a 'cheerful rebel'!

Here again he accepts that weakness and failure will always be part of the monastic life. The Abbot, like the good manager, should be beside the weak, especially when facing the consequences of their failure. Failure, then, is not a moment of defeat for the monk or for his Abbot: it is a moment of renewed confidence, and new resolutions. That is why the system of discipline in Benedict's Rule lays so much stress on forgiveness.

This may not always be possible in business – indeed, tolerance may be limited when targets are not met or rules broken. But in every business there has to be a sense of community, in which the give and take between colleagues allows for both forgiveness and reconciliation.

This story makes us reflect on how we should treat one group of people who have grown up with few of the supports in our society.

Getmerich was born into a deprived family at the heart of an old industrial city. His father spent more years in prison than supporting the family, his mother was a prostitute. Getmerich was a bit of a surprise to his parents. He was given this eccentric name to show they had a sense of humour; they wanted to give the baby hope for the future.

His father's criminal activities did not amount to much: continual, persistent and incurable kleptomania. He would steal anything, eventually get caught and be sentenced to time in prison. The local police would pretend to think it was someone else and eventually come to his house and knock on the door. He admitted his guilt at once. And if he denied it, they accepted his word. Getmerich did not have much chance; he inherited the best and the worst from both parents.

Quick-witted rather than intelligent, he had immense charm, a fine sense of humour and was good company. He inherited his father's weakness, kleptomania, active from his early teens. Inevitably he spent time 'inside', but somehow he managed to come out with a big smile across his face and appear to be no worse for the experience.

After a little schooling he managed to charm his way into jobs, eventually settling to the job of door-keeper to one of the bigger hotels in the area. He was outstandingly good at it, always smiling, able to welcome everyone as they arrived and especially kind to the lame and the elderly, carrying their bags and helping them up the steps. The hotel manager thought the world of him. He knew also that every so often Getmerich would be away for a few months, 'doing time', but since these things happened during his time off and never involved anyone at the hotel, he was able to keep him in post. Getmerich was thrilled with this. His work brought the best out of him. When visitors were asked to comment on their stay, many highlighted the kindness and consideration of the man at the door. He was a real asset.

Then a serious event happened. Some in the 'underworld' were jealous of his success at the hotel, and decided to pull him down a peg. They decided to ambush him one night on his way back from work, and beat him up. Unfortunately, in the brawl, Getmerich took out his knife to defend himself. In the emotion of the moment he thrust the knife at anyone who came near, made contact with one of his attackers and knifed him in the heart. He died soon after.

The case hit the headlines; Getmerich was up for murder, subsequently reduced to manslaughter, and was sent down for five years. This was something he had not expected. Given the tight loyalties in the underworld, few came to his defence; he felt isolated. To make matters worse, the press discovered where he worked. The news headlines highlighted the doorman of the hotel as the man convicted of manslaughter and sent to prison.

In prison Getmerich received a supportive letter from the management, but he felt he would never get his job back. The months and years ticked by as he served his term. The prison experience was much worse than it had been for his petty thieving, and he found the hardened criminals difficult to take. No one from the hotel came to visit him.

On discharge he went home, got himself dressed and went back to the manager of the hotel to see whether he could get his job back. Should he give it him back?

If the story had been centred not on a hotel, but on a monastic guesthouse, I am sure most Abbots would take Getmerich back and eventually return him to his old job.

But we ask: should the hotel management act differently?

Should they not be able to present a case for a phased re-introduction of Getmerich without any sense of embarrassment or concern for negative coverage? There is, after all, plenty to build the case on: the cards were stacked against him from the start, and he had an outstanding record with working at the hotel. Surely all of us recognize an obligation to support those who have failed? We must, at least, try to avoid pushing them back into failure. There will be a risk: a courageous manager will accept it.

Fourth piece of advice: *to be a teacher you must first of all be a disciple of the word of the One Teacher.* If you live what you teach, fear not to repeat yourself in what you say: it will never be the same. Your teaching must be formative and with a view to transformation; if you only inform, you do not form.

I was struck once when visiting a prestigious bank to be taken, as part of the tour, to the prayer room. It was not a specifically Christian place, indeed it was the sort of quiet but nondescript room where anyone of any faith or none could come and be silent. I was struck because I had not expected it. The computers, the conversation about bank rates, exchange rates and reserves, were far from spiritual. I asked the guide whether the room was used. He assured me it was used frequently by senior executives and recently-joined secretaries. It was there, he assured me, to provide a place of quiet where anyone could reflect, stand back from stress, and be able to order thoughts prior to important decision-making.

So, I wondered, was there really such a big gap between the monastery, where the monks pray for inspiration, and the commercial world where the company provides in that place an atmosphere which allows time and silence for people to be, reflect and, perhaps, pray. For the monk, and for the banker too, the experience of prayer brings a sense of powerlessness which helps us gain a better perspective on daily living.

If business is to be the proper fabric in our society, then it needs to be underpinned by personal integrity of those in

senior management. Such integrity demands 'another dimension' and it is precisely that which Benedict demands of the
Abbot. This may offer encouragement to those in business.

Alongside the busy-ness of each day there should be
moments for silence, reflection and, perhaps, for prayer. That
is not just a monastic way, to personal integrity: it is the way
of any one who takes the spiritual dimension seriously.

This story shows how, even in charity, it is easy to get priorities mixed. It helps us to reflect on how we might act.

Sara is intelligent, courageous and energetic. She trained as
an engineer, first getting a good degree and then successfully completing postgraduate studies in Drainage,
Irrigation, and Water Engineering. She always wanted to
work in the developing world. She was taken on by an aid
agency with strong Christian principles, among which was
a commitment to teetotalism. She did not mind that herself
– they did not force their employees to be teetotal. She was
assigned to work on projects in Africa.

She had been in the job for ten years and had established a good reputation, being particularly effective in the
field, with a talent for getting projects started and ensuring
they kept working. Her speciality . . . plants for pumping
and treating water.

Her first love is working in the most remote areas.
There she finds the people charming and co-operative, while
the distance from supplies tests her ingenuity and versatil-
ity. She has learned many local languages and this enables
her to keep in touch during those critical months after she
has finished the installation. Most of her projects give little
trouble.

The more she lives among these people, the more she
appreciates their customs and kindness. At the same time,

she is aware of the destruction caused by the HIV/AIDS virus. She worries that this will undermine all the good her aid agency has done.

Because the aid agency requires her to keep the donors informed of what is happening on the ground, she travels frequently between Europe and Africa. On one return journey she found herself caught in the customs. She knew they could be difficult, but she had, over the years, devised ways of getting round difficult officials.

She was bringing in precious drugs for HIV victims and was hoping that a consignment of water pumps, worth about £1 million, would have arrived a few days before. She hoped to get both items through the customs at the same time. She declared the drugs as gifts for the mission. But the officer demanded a huge bribe to let her through. She could not possibly meet the bribe and refused to co-operate. Nothing happened; no approval, no disapproval. After half an hour, the request was repeated and again she turned it down. After five hours the bribe had been reduced considerably and she felt she could pay it.

Having got through she went in search of the water pumps. Having found them, she discovered the problems were even more acute. She decided to go into the town, find a bed for the night, and return the next day. She made a few phone calls during the night to the aid agency and spoke to others she knew. The country, she was advised, is moving into chaos. She should proceed carefully.

Next day she returned to the customs office in order to start the process. Getting the first set of forms and going to find the first signature, she was met by a couple of officials, clearly angry at her request. As expected, they demanded a bribe before doing anything. She would not agree.

She considered the options: to sit tight and let things

cool down because things might be better in a few days, or to
make representation to the government asking them to
intervene; after all, the equipment was for the good of the
country. Or should she report the matter to headquarters
and let them sort it out? But bringing pressure from abroad
might precipitate an even worse situation; Sara might be
expelled and the machines confiscated because the aid
agency had misrepresented the country in the overseas
media, thus damaging what exports and tourism the
country still had.

She went for an imaginative option. She knew the
people had a weakness for Western spirits, most especially
whisky. She bought a case of fine whisky and a case of fine
brandy. She made the offer to the official; the pumps were on
her lorry within fifteen minutes.

But she had broken a fundamental principle of the aid
agency. Her success soon got out and news spread rapidly,
both praising her bold and imaginative thinking and highlighting the feebleness of the aid agency's commitment to
teetotalism. The issue reached the national press in the UK.

The aid agency was not too pleased. What should
they do?

*Can I work
in this business?*

7

Sharing the Burdens

Anthony Marett-Crosby

Benedict's Abbots are truly in charge of their communities. This is not something Benedict tries to conceal behind any vague talk of sharing leadership: so he states:

> It is best, in the interest of preserving peace and charity, that the authority for the whole of the administration of the monastery should rest with the Abbot. (RB 65)

This may be highly unfashionable in a business context. Yet there is in the Rule plenty of delegation, and a whole host of officials who play key roles in the monastery, exercising a stewardship proper to them. Benedict allows for a Prior, second to the Abbot, to whom is entrusted much of the administration of monasteries in modern communities. Monks responsible for the care of the sick and of guests are important because they have direct contact with those in whom Christ is specially to be seen. But those with responsibility for material goods are not despised – far from it. The principle is clear:

> This superior should entrust the property of the monastery consisting in tools, clothing or any other

items to various members of the community whose
character and reliability inspire confidence. (RB 32)

This is a sharing of the burden of care, but it is not the
creation of miniature Abbots over each department. Because
all other roles come from the Abbot, no authority belongs to
anyone else as of right.

This chapter will proceed by way of two case studies drawn
from the Rule. The first to be examined is that of the most difficult delegation – the care of the whole community to the
Prior. This is a section in which Benedict explores the opportunities and threats arising from substantive delegation, not
just from asking someone else to post a letter. The second case
study concerns the Cellarer, the monk responsible for the
care of all the physical and material goods of the monastery.
A briefer examination of the role of the Cellarer reveals
something of what lies at the heart of this theme in the Rule.

The second in command

It is in Chapter 65 of the Rule, where Benedict discusses the
office of Prior, that his model of delegation is most fully
explored. Unusually, the chapter on the Prior starts not with
the opportunities or the principles, but with the risk. Because
of the weight of tradition coming before Benedict, he notes
that the appointment of a Prior, as of any Number Two, can
cause serious problems within the community. Benedict here
cites his own experience, though he gives us no details of
what he had encountered. Nevertheless, he speaks of the
'grave scandal' that can be caused by a Prior in the
monastery. The reason for this is quite explicit:

There have been instances where some of these
officials have conceived out of an evil spirit of self-
importance that they are like second Abbots, and for

that reason they have assumed the powers of a tyrant,
so that they encourage scandalous divisions in a community. (RB 65)

This is powerful language. Why is such a problem envisaged
here? It might be argued that divergence within the community
could enable people with different skills and temperaments to
perform at their best. Benedict does not see it this way at all –
right at the beginning of the Rule, in his prologue, he establishes
the unity of the community founded upon their common call
from the one God. He talks there about the community pro-
gressing as a whole along the monastic way of life and in faith,
language which he amplifies at the end of the Rule, when he
speaks of the mutual obedience which ties the community
together, in the way 'that will take them straight to God'.

Yet Benedict is here making a more subtle point than the
dangers of divided authority. He certainly has had experience
of monasteries where the conduct of the Prior has been a
cause of difficulty, but more fundamentally, Benedict sees the
Prior as the victim rather than the cause of the trouble. The
real problem lies in the way in which the Number Two is
appointed. So he writes:

This sort of thing is most likely to happen . . . where
the Prior is appointed by the same Bishop or priest
who appointed the Abbot or Abbess. (RB 65)

Benedict describes such an arrangement as absurd, a word
he uses very rarely and very seriously. He sees any such
system of appointment as fatally flawed, since it inevitably
implies an equality between Abbot and Prior, that exempts
the Prior from the Abbot's authority.

This is the antithesis of the model of leadership in the
Rule. In the first place, such a situation threatens those who
lead. Because Benedict sees all people as of value, he applies

this even to leaders, whose first responsibility is, as monks, for the integrity of their own journey to God. This is gravely threatened if, as Benedict envisages, there comes a situation where the Prior is independent of the authority of the Abbot. For Benedict, this places 'their own souls at risk', precisely in contrast to the principle enunciated with regard to the Abbot, who teaches not only by word but by his own experience of journeying towards God.

In the second place, this structure imperils the whole community because it encourages the monks to take sides. This 'brings ruin on them too', because it denies the basic willingness to value even those with whom we disagree. One of the striking things in Benedict's chapter on community decision-making is that all should be heard. But once a group of people has taken sides, listening stops. We assume we know what they say, and we always assume the worst.

Theory and practice

Having said all this, it is a wonder that Benedict thinks having a second in command is worth trying at all. In fact, this is the model of government to which he gives the most space within the Rule. Having explored the risk, Benedict then establishes three important principles which enable delegation, but at the same time preserve peace and charity.

The first principle is that the authority to make decisions should ultimately rest in one place. What he does not mean by delegation is that individual monks gain entirely separate kingdoms, in which they function as some kind of Abbot in miniature. There is only one Abbot, and only one person should take that title.

At the same time, Benedict establishes that power should be delegated to as many people as possible:

> Since power is delegated to many, there is no room for
> pride to take hold of any individual. (RB 65)

Pride here refers to a sense of independence, to being in charge on one's own and, more dangerously, for one's self. The system of Deans, monks in charge of groups of ten others, achieves this by a structure of parallel delegation:

> To take care of all the needs of the groups of ten placed under them and to do so in all respects in accordance with God's commandments and the instructions of their superior. (RB 21)

This duty of care is at once spiritual and material. We hear of Deans being appointed to supervise the monks at different times of the day, but they are called also to know their group well enough that the Abbot may share with them the burden of guiding souls.

This model of co-responsibility may seem very attractive, and Benedict is not including it in his Rule just for fun. It had a long tradition in monastic life, and Benedict valued it. However, he gives far more space to the pattern in which the Abbot has, immediately beneath him, a Prior. The need for this is not based on theory but on practice. He speaks of local needs dictating such a structure, and even of the community requesting it of the Abbot.

The actual responsibility of the second in command is not given precise definition by Benedict. It is part of his wisdom that he leaves such details in the hands of particular Abbots, because particular local situations really matter, and should be taken into account even at the level of major delegation structures. All Benedict says is that the Prior:

> Must carry out the duties delegated to him with due respect for the superior, against whose express wishes nothing must be attempted. (RB 65)

The fact that Benedict conceived of this overall second in command as a responsible official is seen when he echoes advice already given to the Abbot. As we have seen, the Abbot was called upon to lead his community by a 'two-fold calling', in other words, that his life was to teach as much as his words. The same is true for the Prior, who by virtue of his position:

> The greater must be his devotion to the observance of the Rule. (RB 65)

When things go wrong, again
It may seem depressing that Benedict concludes this portrait of the Prior by harking back to the point he has already made, the danger that things might go wrong. He does the same with the Deans, ending that chapter on another down note:

> If any of the deans are affected by some breath of pride which lays them open to adverse criticism, they should be corrected once or twice or even three times. After that, if any are unwilling to change for the better, they should be deposed from their position of responsibility. (RB 21)

For the Prior, this structure is repeated, although a fourth warning is added. After this, the Prior is to be made subject to the discipline of the Rule and then dismissed. With regard to the Prior, there is even a further stage, that:

> If a dismissed Prior cannot live in peace and obedience in the monastery, then they must be expelled. (RB 65)

At first sight, this seems to function as a kind of red light, highlighting the dangers of delegation. In fact, in the context of the rest of the Rule, Benedict is saying that the Deans, and even more the Prior, are to be given more of an opportunity to get things wrong and then change than any other monk. With no one else does Benedict allow four verbal warnings coming before the discipline of the Rule is applied.

What is suggested here is an awareness that delegation brings risk and an opportunity to learn. Not even the best Prior in the world is made such from the womb. He has to discover what it means to take on this responsibility, and how best to work with a particular Abbot. Benedict wants there to be time for this to happen.

Like a father

Where Benedict is hesitant with regard to creating a second in command in the shape of the Prior, he has absolutely no reluctance in upholding the necessity of someone to whom the Abbot can delegate the responsibility for the material goods of the monastery. In monastic tradition, this figure is named the Cellarer, and there was a long history of such people playing an important part in the daily life of monasteries from well before Benedict's own day. Whereas with the Prior, Benedict was striking out on his own, with the Cellarer he is reflecting the wisdom that had accumulated, as well as taking it forward a step or two. Chapter 31 of the Rule, which offers Benedict's vision for the Cellarer, is one of the most carefully crafted and poised chapters in the whole text – none of it is trying to be radical, to change the face of monastic delegation. Rather, he is presenting a careful synthesis, new in some subtle ways, of a figure without whom monasteries would simply cease to function.

This is probably the first and most important point of all. The Cellarer is essential to the daily functioning of the monastery, and there is nothing in the Rule which suggests that the Abbot should take on the task for himself. But Benedict goes on to describe someone who is not only essential, but also is a benefit to the community. Dealing with material things and the complexities of the daily running of the community is not a necessary evil, but an opportunity to do good. Indeed, the Cellarer is the only person apart from the Abbot to whom Benedict gives the title 'Father'.

So a large part of Chapter 31 of the Rule is taken up with a list of qualities. It is at first sight a rather random collection of admirable character traits. Read this quotation, and count up how many people you know who fit into this description:

> To qualify for this choice a candidate should be wise and mature in behaviour, sober and not an excessive eater, not proud nor apt to give offence nor inclined to cause trouble, not unpunctual, nor wasteful but living in the fear of God and ready to show the community love. (RB 31)

If that were an advertisement for an upcoming job in any organization, the number of honest applicants would be quite small. Benedict knows this well – a lot of what we have seen already in the Rule emphasizes his willingness to see people as they are, to recognize their strengths and weaknesses in an honest but positive way. So where does this list come from?

Benedict expects the monastic readers of his Rule to recognize it straight away. It is drawn from the New Testament, and specifically from the lists of qualities which New Testament writers wanted to see in those called to Christian leadership and service in the ministry of the deacon. The word 'deacon' is Greek for servant, and therein lies the point. All these qualities are meant to place the Cellarer in the context of Christian service. That is what this job is really about, and to understand it in any other terms is to misinterpret it dangerously.

This is summarized in the pair of qualities with which Benedict ends his list. They are not drawn from the New

. . . the number of honest applicants would be quite small.

Testament image of the deacon, and again, Benedict would expect his monks to know that. They form Benedict's commentary on the list from the tradition, a double commandment which makes sense of all the practical arrangements with which the rest of the chapter is concerned. On the one side lies the fear of God, the daily remembering that what is done in the monastery can and should be a sign of the God for whom monks undertake their life. On the other hand is the command to make manifest that most God-like of virtues, love. In a remarkable conclusion to this 'job description', Benedict writes that the Cellarer should:

> Be ready to show the community all the love a Father
> or Mother would show to their family. (RB 31.2)

This is hugely powerful language – delegation and responsibility are taken quite outside the institutional framework within which we would normally understand them. In fact, the institutional mentality is here shown to be a snare, a distraction from the real business of making people feel part of a family.

The key word in Benedict's description of the Cellarer is 'care'. It is a concept that Benedict uses sparingly in the Rule as a whole, except in terms of the duty that the monastery has towards the sick, the young and the old. Here, that duty towards people on the margins of a community is extended in two striking ways. First, the Cellarer's task is to look to the care of the physical goods of the monastery. This is the point when Benedict stresses most clearly the potential that all things have to do good, and the consequent duty to protect and nourish them. There is not a hint of disdain for the things of this world – quite the opposite.

But the Cellarer has another duty of care, without which the former would become mere administration. Benedict makes clear that the highest duty of this subordinate is to exercise care for the brethren. Remember that Benedict's monks own nothing and, like all people without the security of material goods, they are exposed to risk. The Cellarer is presented as the barrier between this risk and the necessary security which enables a monk to do his job properly. In a sense, everything depends on him. Therefore it cannot be enough to focus simply on the Cellarer's duty towards things, however exulted this might be. He wants the care of people to be the reason why the Cellarer cares for things.

The particular example that Benedict takes of this kind of approach is immediately familiar to anybody who has been in any position of leadership. It is always easy to be a leader when things go well, when all we have to do is to say 'Yes'. But when someone comes with a request that we cannot meet, then saying 'No' can hurt. There is the danger that refusing looks and feels like devaluing or ignoring the one who makes the request. No one who was ready to accede to every request, could ever be a monastic Cellarer, but Benedict lays down a way of saying 'No' that avoids personal rejection and instead aims at strengthening the individual even at this difficult moment.

> A refusal of a request should be measured and given
> with due deference towards the person involved . . .
> Among the most important qualities the Cellarer
> needs to cultivate his humility and the ability to give
> a pleasant answer even when a request must be
> refused. (RB 31)

We might note the two obvious points Benedict is making here. The first is that the person asking probably does not know as much as the person refusing, and the reply given should acknowledge the fact. This is part of what Benedict means by measure, an awareness that the individual is probably not being deliberately outrageous or stupid. Such an openness towards the good intentions of the other then leads into the second quality, deference. This means that the person who receives the refusal deserves a reason, simply because of who that person is. What, in short, Benedict is laying down is a vision for dialogue even at a moment of refusal.

In taking the Prior and the Cellarer as two case studies in delegation in the Rule, we are focusing inevitably upon the top jobs. The reason for this is fairly obvious – if these are got right, then there is at least a chance that those responsibilities that flow from them will also be about right. Benedict lays down the possibility, perhaps even the necessity, that under these officials there will be others who share in the duty of stewardship. Thus, at the end of the chapter on the Cellarer he writes:

> If the community is large, the Cellarer must receive the assistance of helpers whose support will make the burden of this office tolerable. (RB 31)

Delegation as stewardship, delegation as support: these seem to be the key phrases that Benedict is using throughout the chapters we have looked at. Of all the qualities of the Abbot, it is stewardship that really can be delegated – perhaps that *must* be delegated. The other attributes of leadership belong, for better or worse, to the one so chosen, and to delegate these would be meaningless, possibly even dangerous. The duty of care is placed on the shoulders of all, and the exercise of this care for the sake of others comes very close to being Benedict's way to God.

8

Working Together

Kit Dollard

Something special happens when two or more people start working together. It is a bit like an orchestra: '95 per cent of the time when we are playing it is good music but every now and then, something magical happens that transcends human understanding and lifts the listeners into a different world,' says the leader of a national orchestra. Working together is also one of the great hopes for marriage, that $1 + 1 = 3$, or 4, or 5. It is a good analogy because good marriages don't just happen – they require hard work, patience, forgiveness and the whole armoury of virtues. There is also as wide a range and styles of marriages as there are groups of people.

In this chapter we will be talking about how groups of people work together, and specifically we will be talking about teams.

Back to basics

In the 1980s and 90s working in teams was recognized by many businesses as a key element in meeting customer needs, maintaining performance and providing a high level of service. This led to consideration of how to build effective teams. The problem was, and to a degree it still is, that most people recognize the need but are unsure of what team building involves, and indeed question the benefit of spending time and money pursuing the goals of building a strong team.

In reality, groups or teams of people often happen automatically at work, without formal procedures – it is just that we seldom use this as a way of operating. Informal groups almost always arise if the opportunities exist.

But first, what is a team? There are many definitions of a team, but the one that is most useful (and the shortest!) is *'a group of people working together towards a common goal'*. However, this definition throws up more questions. First, how many are in the group? There is room for discussion here – Belbin says that six is the ideal number, but others vary between four and twelve. It is interesting that in practice Benedictine communities do not get much smaller than six.

Second, why is working together so important? Why can't Benedict's followers just be together and pray – after all isn't that what monks are supposed to do? Well, yes – to a point, but Benedict is very keen on his followers working! Chapter 48, one of the longer chapters in the Rule, starts with the warning 'Idleness is the enemy of the soul' and then goes on to lay down instructions about how the work is to be done – divided into physical, mental and spiritual activity. We also read of the concept that no one is to overwork. So there is balance in the proposals, but the principles are quite clear. The important thing for Benedict is that his followers work *together*. This is part of the reason why he regards the cenobite as the strongest type of monk and why the sarabaite and the gyrovague are to be avoided. Benedict has recognized that when people work together it creates climates of support and trust and, most important of all, it builds respect.

Third, what is the common aim? In many businesses it is easily recognizable – to increase the sales of the company, to produce a world-beating cancer drug, or to safeguard shareholders' interests – but although the goal may be recognizable, the difficulty sometimes appears to be in translating this into the 'How to'. That explains the rush, some years ago, to produce mission statements. Teachers, solicitors, doctors, dentists and university lecturers all bent their minds to producing, in a few short sentences, the goal or purpose of their work. In retrospect, most people agree that the results, though admirable, only serve to illustrate the gap between reality and desire. Many company employees, if asked to identify their company's mission, will get it wrong or say it is irrelevant to their own area of responsibility.

'The trouble with mission statements is that they are produced by the management and have very little relevance to those of us who actually have to deal with customers,' said Mary-Clare, an executive in a stationery company. 'They (the management) assume that all customers want to buy our services, they do not recognize that in many instances it requires a lot of selling. That usually ends up on my plate and I feel that I just do not have the skills, the time or the commitment. I think we need to completely re-think our mission statement, and this time to involve everybody in the firm. In that way we might start working together rather than as five different departments.'

Perhaps this is one area where Benedict has an advantage. Everyone who becomes involved in the slightest way with Benedict follows a common goal. Monastics take formal vows, and even the visitor to a monastery taking part in the Office of the Day is committed to a common goal for that period of time. It would be inspiring if everybody who became involved with our businesses – whether as customers, suppliers or employees – understood our common goal. It would certainly save discussions, arguments and even court cases. Perhaps we only have ourselves to blame for not making our mission statements relevant, clear and visionary.

> Richard is the Chairman of a small chain of supermarkets in the south west of England. 'If you do not know where you are going then any road will take you there. I am a firm believer in a common statement of intent, or mission statement. It took us about six months to work ours out, but everybody now understands what we are trying to do. It is posted above every cash register, every vehicle and on every piece of stationery. It is only one sentence and is very simple: "We are here to serve you."'

In Chapter 11 we will explore how Benedict links hospitality or customer service to moving people to a more common sense of purpose or mission.

The life cycle of a team

All teams have life cycles. A common description is five phases – forming, storming, norming, performing and mourning.

This life cycle is no more than an acceptance of group dynamics and that things change when people work together in groups. Benedict too recognizes that people working together tire, and if they are to continue to function at their best they need encouragement. That is why he urges his followers to look to the other person when times are tough (like the early morning!).

In the morning . . . they should quietly give encouragement to those who are sleepy and given to making
excuses for being late. (RB 22.8).

And again the value of communication between individuals:

. . . a kindly word is of greater value than a gift,
however precious. (RB 32.14)

Seriously good teams

In the 1980s Belbin – among others – experimented with
trying to find the ideal team. His experiments with the 'Apollo
teams', which comprised the most clever people and consistently failed to do well in business simulations exercises, led
to an acknowledgement that people behaved in a different
way in groups and that it did not always depend on their
innate gifts. Many others have tried to analyse the make-up
of the most successful teams in businesses, and listed below
is a representative sample from the many thinkers on team
management. It includes many of the different qualities that
might go into a well-functioning team:

- Shared objective and goals.
- A climate of support and trust and acceptance of weak-
  nesses.
- Open lines of communication.
- Clear procedures – especially when matters go wrong.
- Appropriate leadership.
- Recognition that conflict is inevitable.
- A process of feedback or review.
- The ability to relate positively to other groups.

Certainly it is possible to discuss and add or subtract to this
list, but it is a good starting-point from which to start a conversation with Benedict.

Some more scientific team-building models

Psychometric instruments (measurement of the mind) are today providing an objective standpoint from which to regard the world of the mind. They are a map or chart from which it is possible to survey the almost never-ending vista of the human mind and personality. They should be regarded as no more or less than this. However, it is worth examining their role, because at first sight they may have little to say to Benedict, but they have come to play an increasingly important part in helping businesses to understand people, and teams in particular. Myers Briggs, Margreson, Belbin and more recently S. P. Myers have all contributed significantly, and it is worth trying to analyse whether Benedict has anything more to add or confirm in this conversation.

If you are a practising Christian, especially a practising Catholic, you might feel that this is all very unorthodox, but before you dismiss this whole way of thinking it is worth reflecting on 'Church in the Modern World', one of the four major documents that came from the Second Vatican Council which ran from 1962 for five years and must rank as one of the great events of the Christian world. It declares that 'In pastoral care sufficient use should be made, not only of theological principles, but also of the findings of secular sciences, especially psychology and sociology.'

The basic concepts that have emerged from the thinkers above, and upon which all could probably agree, are:

- There is a difference between a team role (that person's ability to behave, contribute and interact with others in a particular way) and a team function (what a team member does in response to specific technical demands placed upon them, i.e. competence and experience).
- All team roles are equal.

- Winning teams comprise the best mixture of team role and team function.
- Each task and team will be different.
- A team takes on a life of its own.

Here is an example to illustrate this:

Judy is an interpersonal skills training specialist with a large multinational company. 'Last week we had to give our presentational skills refresher course to the regional directors. I delivered exactly the same material five times during the week and every time it was a totally different experience. The group dynamics were just completely different. On one day we went off on tangents about identifying needs through questions techniques, but on another, we spent all the session and our energy on talking about selling techniques through NLP. It might have been five different firms.'

A look at the dynamics of Benedict's skills for working together

If we look to Benedict for how to work together, it is possible to put them into three areas – similar to Adair's team needs:

God   The Abbot   Each other (individuals)

The first two are discussed in other chapters, so we will focus on individuals.

The key to working – and developing – successful teams must centre on the qualities of the team members. People are difficult to replicate and this forces us to focus on developing and nurturing team members. Central to this are qualities of respect or trust and equality.

Mutual respect and support for the individual
The first essential quality is what Benedict describes as a good spirit:

> It is this spirit that all should strive to cultivate . . . they should try to be the first to show respect to one another with the greatest patience in tolerating weaknesses of body or character. (RB 72.3–6)

We met this attitude earlier and it is part of good zeal. Benedict says that there is a need to respect each other, and this is surely the critical quality in working with others. But he goes further than this when he commands the greatest patience in tolerating weaknesses. This can sometimes result in the most testing of situations, and it is the leader's duty to ensure that the weakest in the team is looked after.

More than respect there is equality
There is always a middle line in dealing with the frailties of people in groups, and Benedict is quick to accept this:

> Distribution is made according to each in accordance with their needs. This however should not be taken to mean that favouritism of individuals can be tolerated; far from it. (RB 34.2)

and then he goes on to outline the proper attitude:

> Those who do not need as much as some others should thank God for the strength they have been given and not be sorry for themselves. Those who need more should be humble about their weaknesses and not become self-important in enjoying the indulgence granted them. (RB 34.5)

There is a real message here for successful teams – particularly in the performing stage when personalities have begun to exert themselves. The real team player has the characteristics above – in some way they are able to think beyond their own gifts ands skills and see the advantage of trying to use the talents of even the weakest member. It is the skill of making everybody participate in the common aim.

Internal communication as key

Finally, a word about communication. The most common cause of breakdown in business relationships between people is communication. It is always a two-way process, and an important element in the manager's toolkit. In the old days, a printed news-sheet of company social events and 'matches, hatches and despatches' of employees was sufficient. Today, the whole range of communication tools needs to be used, from closed e-mail newsgroups to 'one-minute manager'-style conversations.

It is difficult to measure the value of induction days, regular team meetings, celebrations and in-house training events, which not only put over the values and 'personality' of the organization but also allow the managers to listen to the employees. It is an opportunity for the two-way process of communication to occur.

It is no accident that Benedict begins his Rule with the words 'Listen'. Central to the theme of treating every person as an individual is the need to listen – perhaps Benedict's most well-known command. Listening is the quality that produces trust. It is time-consuming and tiring, but it is the key to personal growth and development – as any parent will tell you.

In the Western world we take in 82 per cent of our information through our eyes, 11 per cent through our ears and 7 per cent through our other senses. Sometimes we regard listening as hearing, and it is only after a failed conversation that we recognize they are not the same. We can train ourselves to be better listeners – and for better relationships, it is essential.

9

The Abbot Reflects . . .

You may feel that Anthony and Kit are talking about two different things, and it is not clear how either helps to answer the question 'Can I work in this business?'. In a sense, this is an accurate reflection of some monasteries, and possibly some businesses too!

What we have here are three aspects of organization: teamwork, leadership and delegation. But each is examined from one perspective, either that of business or from Benedict. In fact, no organization can function smoothly without a sense of teamwork, as Kit has explored. On the other hand, Anthony has concentrated on what Benedict says about the Prior and the Cellarer, two of the most important functions in the monastery.

If the organization you have set up functions well, it will also function well in your absence. Wisdom that stems from experience will allow you to be a good administrator and avoid these possible obstacles: servile dependence on experts; absolute confidence in organizations; waiting for science to confirm what common sense makes evident to you.

This advice relates directly to what this section is trying to explore, a business in which it is a pleasure to work.

Let me start with a word about the 'team', frequently used as a way of bringing people together so that their combined efforts can be successful. The team, as Kit has shown, is focused on a goal. Our sports-mad world shows its importance – hard work in training is geared for the game or the season. But once over, what is left? Some friends, perhaps a silver cup on the mantelpiece, and a few memories. A lot of work goes into team building for something that lasts a short time.

The same might be said of business: teams are built to perform a function, whether it is car assembly or to pursue a legal case. The need for communication, for awareness, for mutual support is self-evident, and the life cycle, as described by Kit, shows its impermanence: 'forming, storming, norming, performing, mourning'. No one has a permanent place in a 'team'.

So perhaps the challenge is to change a team into a community. Many of us would like to work in a business which is a community rather than face the hectic life of forming and re-forming teams. In community we would find stability and a sense of purpose which lasts longer.

We have discussed the matter of leadership in community and business, but the role of the Number Two or deputy is particularly important to promote continuity and safeguard unity. As Anthony has shown, Benedict faced a dilemma about this. The Prior was, in some monasteries, appointed by someone other than the Abbot, an arrangement that led to division. No one in business will be surprised at this. A Number Two has to work closely with his superior, but all recognize that it is only natural for one to feel under threat from the subordinate, while the subordinate might dream of eventually being in charge. This natural state of affairs has to be watched.

If Benedict had been writing for a more modern audience he could not have provided a better job description for the Prior, the loyal Number Two, who sees to the smooth working of the community, defending the Abbot whether he agrees with him or not, available to the brethren, listening patiently to their complaints and bearing all with humour. Each Abbot longs for the Prior who is his complement; two of the same type would make life impossible for the brethren, but different characters with a little bit of age difference bring out the best in what has to be the most important relationship in the community. There is something here which may be relevant to other organizations.

The well-run monastery, like the well-run business, depends on delegation, and the sure test is whether it functions as smoothly when the boss is away. This depends on the wisdom that comes with experience. Friction can arise so easily when senior management is divided, or the Prior or bursar are taking a different line from the Abbot. Anthony has shown the importance of the bursar in Benedict's scheme. He conforms more to the experienced business manager than either the Abbot or Prior.

In the following story we show how a particularly skilled person managed to get herself and her business into difficulties because she lacked the proper advice at the right moment.

Lilac is 68 and something of a force to be reckoned with in her town. She trained many years ago as a hairdresser and hair stylist, and developed such a real talent that she soon had her own business and numerous people coming to train under her. She was 'the' place in the town to have one's hair done, and of course it was the centre of all the town's gossip.

Lilac revelled in her position of being the unofficial opinion-former in the area. And Lilac had views on many things way beyond types of hair and colour and styles. After 40 years of dedicated work she was an 'institution' in her own right; all elected politicians, or anyone who sought to get elected, trod the path to her salon, to seek her approval. Her views were firmly held and forcefully expressed. Having one's hair done in her salon was not just a matter of having one's appearance renewed, but a moment of education and enrichment.

Lilac lived life to the full. Outside her work she lived well and entertained lavishly. Although the business thrived, she had a penchant for spending, and those closest to her had fears for the security of her finances in the longer term. Her husband, whom she adored, had been able to look after her finances. Sadly he had died from cancer three years earlier. She found herself without a guide in this crucial area.

Her spending increased, but income remained static. What capital she had was being eroded away. For the business, she had professional accountants and she asked one of them for advice. He advised her to find someone to buy the business, but continue to employ her. This would give her a capital sum and a guaranteed income. The capital sum would help to shore up her pension, and the income would allow her to continue to live in the style she was used to.

A buyer was found, a lady of equal reputation in London, who wanted to expand by taking over establishments of similar prestige. It seemed an excellent fit, because the two women appeared to get on well with each other and the arrangement seemed to guarantee success. A sum was agreed, the lawyers sorted out the details and the deal was formalized, with much rejoicing. Lilac's loyal supporters, aware that age was creeping up, thought they had gained a very suitable replacement.

But, as so often, the fine print of the agreement was not worked out in detail and an important issue was left out: the date of Lilac's retirement. It was assumed that she would go at 65. Her sixty-fifth birthday came and went. She made no mention of retirement.

Something else started to happen. It was clear that old age was having its effect – the excitement of her presence was dulled, her skill started to diminish and an air of anxiety hovered over the salon. The question on everyone's lips was: 'Is Lilac over the top?'

The new owner was not happy with this state of affairs. Custom falling away, albeit slowly, meant the huge sum she had to borrow to pay for the business was not getting paid back at the planned rate. The answer was clear: change was needed before things got too bad. Lilac had to retire – but how ?

This needed to be handled with great care: the situation was precarious enough. Lilac, given all that she has achieved, her reputation and the position she holds, is not going to retire easily. Old people in this position tend to cling to their positions: they cannot bear the thought of living obscurely and having to endure the inactivity that comes with it.

As a major attraction in the town, and as key to consumer confidence in the salon, the new owners will have to move slowly and carefully. The worst situation for all concerned would be to have a row in public. The new manager might be tempted to have a 'once-and-for-all set-to', accept there will be a collapse of confidence and then rely on her London reputation to turn it round.

That would be a risk because perceptions are more important to people on the ground than facts. If Lilac is perceived to have been treated unjustly (and it is irrelevant whether she has been or not), then the new business will face great difficulties. Indeed, these difficulties will get worse; Lilac, having been removed from her post in a blazing row, will take refuge in her home and very quickly be writing a column in the local paper, speaking on local radio and appearing on local TV; her message will be critical of the new management. The collapse of confidence will be there for all to see. So it is imperative to get Lilac to retire gracefully.

The problem started with the untimely death of Lilac's husband and her inability to keep track of her affairs. The sale of the business and the falling out with the new owner was always a risk.

To save face on all sides, Lilac could be persuaded to retire gracefully. To do this she has to be elevated both by the new boss and by the town authorities. She needs to be fêted as a celebrity. At the same time, there needs to be a plan to reduce her time in the salon. Perhaps an imaginative trip to places far away, where she could lecture and offer advice, would get her away and help her realize there is another life. She may become a world representative for the business and be encouraged to speak on local radio and TV. She will soon see that this new life keeps her occupied and provides for her retirement.

This little story offers a chance to reflect on how you might deal with a deputy who makes a misjudgement . . .

Brother Angelo was Prior of a small monastery on an island off the west coast. He was 45, and the Abbot ten years older. They were so different in temperament and attitude that they did not get on at all, but each recognized that Brother Angelo was the only candidate for Prior. The monastery was growing but the young monks were insufficiently tested in monastic life to take on the task of being Prior. The Abbot, though he disagreed with Brother Angelo, knew that in heart he was loyal and trustworthy. One matter they disagreed about was the role of the monthly day off. Brother Angelo wanted to return to the practice whereby the monks would leave the monastery and have lunch in a local pub. Father Abbot was dubious about this custom, thinking it put too much temptation in the way of the monks, many of them young and impressionable. He had curtailed the monthly day out. While the Abbot was in Rome at the Congress of Abbots, the Prior decided that he would have the month-day in the local village and allow the brethren to go to the pub. Well, it was such a wonderful day, and the local people were so delighted to see them, that they offered to supplement their meagre rations. The result: three of the young monks had to be carried from the pub, drunk, singing rather unmonastic songs. It became the talk of the island and soon found its way into the press.

How would you advise the Abbot to deal with Brother Angelo, the Prior?

Can I improve my working relationships?

10

Making It Work

Anthony Marett-Crosby

This chapter presents what might be the most recognizably business-centred section of the Rule, dealing with work, skills and planning for the future of the community. Monasteries have always needed to look forward, and they have also needed to live with the real financial demands of the present – ends need to meet, even in religious life. So, having examined the theory that underlies the Rule, we can now turn to explore its nuts and bolts, the attitudes of mind and the practical approaches that hold together the real monastic community in its work.

It is worth repeating that monasteries have always done an amazing variety of different works. Benedict does not say that there is one work proper to monks, except in the rather special sense in which he calls prayer the 'work of God'. Beyond this, Benedict only lays down the principle that monks should work, both because idleness is bad for the soul and also because work has a positive value. It is good because it enables the community to survive, also because it requires monks to work together, to regard each other not just as colleagues in prayer but as people whose skills and abilities make it possible for a monastery to survive. So monks have always worked, whether in the fields of education at all levels, pastoral work, the reception of guests and in the necessary administration that keeps the monastery going. In today's monastic world, work ranges from bee-keeping to creating Internet web pages. One of the points of this book is that Benedict's vision of a community and its work can support any and all of these.

This is where we are

The first step in the process of making the community work, let alone thinking of its future, is a realistic assessment of the present. Benedict wants his Abbot to focus on where the community is by undertaking something like a review of its real assets. For Benedict, these assets are people. So Benedict urges his Abbot to:

> Reflect on what a difficult and demanding task he has accepted, namely that of guiding souls and serving the needs of so many different characters. (RB 2)

Notice the verbs that he uses in this quotation: 'guiding' and 'serving' are Benedict's understanding of what it means to be a leader, immediately bringing back to mind the images of the Abbot as shepherd, healer and steward. This assessment of assets cannot, therefore, be dispassionate – quite the contrary. It is founded on a passion for people, to bring out what is best in the community, once again enabling what is strong to flourish and what is weak to change.

But this is not enough. The recognition of where the community is cannot end, even with the most careful judgement of the strengths and weaknesses of the community. There is always for Benedict something else as well. It is the active God of the present moment which Benedict wants his monks to see first of all, for:

The first step of humility is to cherish at all times the sense of awe with which we should turn to God. It should drive forgetfulness away. (RB 7)

There is a stark reminder of how easy it is to forget to make this kind of assessment in a text we have already met, the *De Consideratione* written by the monastic reformer St Bernard to Pope Eugenius III. Bernard is in the middle of a long section of this book in which he outlines the various failings of the administration. Principal among these is an attitude of mind which may seem all too familiar:

Each day we carefully review our expenses, but are unaware of the steady diminishing of the flock. (*De Consideratione* 4.21)

A monk writing to another monk would expect the echo of the Rule of Benedict in this to be obvious. It raises again the image of the Abbot as shepherd, and invites us to pose a question: what kind of flock are we really most concerned to look after?

Skills and service

There is sometimes a temptation in the Christian life to pretend that all skills and gifts are things we should repress for the sake of God. We can dress this up in all sorts of ways, but in fact this is neither humility nor indeed Christian. Monasteries depend upon the skills of their members, and Benedict writes without hesitation that:

If there are any in the community with gifts, they should use them. (RB 57)

It is of course part of the function of any leader, whether Abbot or anyone else, to call forth these skills from those around him. It would be quite false to the nature of a monastery for anyone to stand back, imagining that one is somehow serving God better by using nothing of what he has. Yet there is a hesitation in Benedict's mind which comes from the way in which the one who is skilled approaches his tasks. What Benedict wants to avoid at all costs is a sense in the mind of the monk that 'without me, this just wouldn't happen'.

Father Alfred was looking forward to his retirement. He had served the monastery for many years, mostly in different administrative roles, supporting successive Abbots as secretary and cellarer. This was regarded by all as an important job, but it had been time-consuming and had been a constant source of distraction and anxiety. So when the Abbot told him that the time had come for a younger man to take on the job, he was relieved. He looked forward to spending time in the community without worrying about the next problem, whether a shortage of money or a flooded bathroom. But after a few weeks of this retirement, he started to find a growing difficulty which proved far more burdensome than any of the worries he had previously had. His successor was doing the job in a completely different way, establishing new priorities, changing long-standing administrative processes and re-structuring systems that Father Alfred had spent many years putting together. The changes irritated him, because they seemed to imply a negative judgement on all that he had done. He found himself prone to becoming angry with his successor, complaining to others about the inadequacy of the new approach, and secretly longing to be back in the harness.

Then he remembered the wise words of the man that he himself had replaced as cellarer many years before. This old father had said something then which Father Alfred, so full of his new job, had hardly noticed. It was this: 'The hardest thing in monastic life is to live with one's successors, to realize that not one of us is essential'.

In many business contexts, this might not happen, since people are promoted, move sideways or change careers, move on or go away. But just ask yourself for a moment what it would feel like, to be eased into retirement and to remain thereafter in day-to-day contact with people doing the very work that you had done, taken pride in and in which you had excelled.

If this feels impossible, or even inhuman, then you are right. It confronts our sense of being necessary, of everything depending upon us getting our desk clear. There are of course times when it is true that we have important things to do; but one day, someone else will do them. This is what Benedict means when, in his chapter on the skills of the community, he emphasizes that they should only ever be done 'with proper humility'. The reverse, of doing a job only because it makes us feel good, is quite the opposite of how Benedict conceives of a community working for each other and with each other. So he writes:

If any of them conceive of an exaggerated idea of their competence . . . imagining that the value of their work puts the monastery in their debt, they should be forbidden further exercise of their skills and not allowed to return to their workshops unless they respond with humility. (RB 57)

Lying behind this understanding of personal skills is some-thing more fundamental. Benedict does not want the value of anyone to be defined or circumscribed by their 'contribution to the community'. This is expressed in some monasteries by a powerful tradition whereby, at the beginning of each year, the whole community gathers before the Abbot or Abbess and each member comes forward to receive his or her duty. Those with important jobs within the monastery join the line with those whose jobs are invisible, or who perhaps are unable to work. To this last group, the Superior says the simple words 'You are the support of the community by your prayers'.

This points towards another basic attitude, that before any question of skill or ability there is an instinct of service. Benedict writes that:

> Everyone in the community should take turns in serving at the table. (RB 35)

It is very much in the process of cooking, eating and clearing up that Benedict sees an opportunity for everyone, however great or small their visible responsibility, to share in an equal task. The reason for this is very straightforward:

> Serving each other in this way has the great merit of fostering charity. (RB 35)

The point about this kind of work is evident: everyone can do it, it is not exciting, and it is a visible form of service. Benedict does allow, as always, for those who might find even this work too difficult. He seems concerned to ensure that as many people as possible should have this opportunity to serve, so he commands that:

> Those who are not very strong should be given assist-ance to make sure that they will not be distressed by the demands of this work. (RB 35)

This kind of undifferentiated service presents every community, be it monastic or business, with a profound challenge. We all become used to dividing one from another in all sorts of subtle ways. A shared service at table is Benedict's way of pointing towards a fundamental equality in the community.

What does this fundamental equality actually mean? We need to be careful here, because it might be read as a levelling down, of ensuring that those at the top don't 'get too big for their boots' by making everybody do something that nobody wants to do at all. It is in fact a way of emphasizing the distinction that must exist in a Benedictine community between vocation and function. It must be the case that the functions of different monks vary both according to the needs of a particular monastery at a particular time and also because of the natural diversity of gifts and skills. To imagine a community where everybody did the same work, undifferentiated by ability, would be to create a monster of quite un-Christian dimensions. But we cannot stop at diversity, for monks are bound together by a common vocation in which everybody shares.

This is why Benedict takes time to construct a community order in such a strange way. There might be all sorts of ways of structuring a community according to age or ability, but Benedict does none of these. He prefers a random approach, where position in the community is determined solely by date of entry. He lays down that:

> All retain the order of their conversion to monastic life
> so exactly that one who arrived at the monastery door
> at the second hour must accept a place junior to
> another who came an hour earlier, whatever their age
> or former rank may have been. (RB 63)

Things and their value

There is no doubt that Benedict values material objects highly. He does not tell his monks to treat the things of this world with disdain, as things to be used and then discarded as if unclean or wicked. In fact he does precisely the opposite, declaring that:

> All the utensils of the monastery and in fact every-
> thing that belongs to the monastery should be cared
> for as though they were the sacred vessels of the altar.
> (RB 31)

Just think about what this implies. The vessels of the altar, to Benedict's mind, are those things so privileged that they can contain God himself – consider what this says about property of the monastery. Each of them, because they can be used for the good of others, becomes in its own way sacramental, that is a means by which God's love and presence can be commu-nicated. Some Christian liturgies have included the custom whereby each vessel of the altar is kissed before it is used, a sign of reverence for something made by human hands for the glory of God. Somehow, Benedict wants us to have the same approach to the mundane things that we use and then are tempted to throw aside when they are no longer needed by us.

When Sister Sue was a very new member of the community, she was set to work in a patch of woodland, and asked to clear some weeds. To do this, she was given a sickle, with which she set to with zeal. She found the process quite fun until, in her enthusiasm, she swung the sickle too hard and it flew out of her hand, out of sight and apparently out of this world. She looked for it with mounting concern, but it never appeared, and she had to go to the novice mistress and to the Abbot to apologize for losing it. It felt a bit like being back at school, and she was inclined to be resentful at having to behave in such an apparently childish way. The real point was brought home to her later, when an old sister to whom she told this story said that she was sorry she had lost the sickle, which 60 years earlier she had used herself. Sister Sue felt she had lost the family silver, and in a sense she had.

This is not just about tradition: it is about stewardship, which is what delegation in the Rule is all about, and the story of Sister Sue shows that this delegation starts straight away. Benedict contrasts this attitude with that of private ownership, which he condemns at every possible opportunity. His chapter on personal possessions stands in radical contradiction to the attitude that most of us, whatever we do, have about the things we have around us:

> It is vitally important to cut out by the roots from the monastery the bad practice of anyone in the community giving away anything or accepting any gift for themselves, as though it were their own personal property . . . After all they cannot count even their bodies and their wills as their own, consecrated as they are to the Lord. (RB 33)

Again, we need to be clear about what Benedict is not saying. He is not despising the things of this world as if beneath the proper attention of his monks. He is inviting us to extend our sense of the possibility for good to the things we use and so frequently abuse.

Risk and opportunity

When it comes down to the practicalities of living and working together, Benedict accepts the possibility of failure. In particular, he identifies a risk which every organization must face: an insidious corrosion from within. Benedict calls this the 'vice of murmuring', the specifically monastic sin. The damage of murmuring is not done by the fact that there is a complaint, but because this complaint is not brought to the attention of anyone who can do anything about it.

Brother Romuald was a man with a grievance. He had noticed a growing tendency for his monastery to be a little more dismissive than they should be of certain kinds of guests, especially of people who just dropped in at the last minute. Travellers, vagrants of various kinds and the poor were welcomed, but only in a rather half-hearted sort of way. The guest master and his assistants were doing good work, but their attitude to this kind of visitor was just not quite right. Brother Romuald could see that clearly, but what he couldn't do was find a way of articulating this concern. He knew it was an important issue, but he did not want to appear to be critical nor did he want to get the job himself. In his monastery, it was always a danger that when you raised a suggestion, it ended up becoming your problem. So, when the Abbot summoned the community to the Chapter, he remained silent, hoping that the problem would go away. Unfortunately it didn't, and nor did his sense of irritation. He found himself unavoidably starting to express his views, but not to anyone who could do anything about it. He started muttering to people in dark corners about how those in authority were neglecting the poor, and thereby ignoring the precept of the Rule. Others agreed

with him, but because it was Romuald's problem, they left it
to him to bring it to the attention of those who could change
it. The guest masters and those in authority were completely unaware of this growing circle of discontent, which
had its root in something good, but which, by the way it was
handled, became viciously bad. Eventually, these mutter-
ings came to the ear of the guest master who felt himself
undermined and abused by this sort of talk. No one was the
winner, and everybody lost, whether guest master, monks or
the poor themselves.

Significantly, Benedict's most powerful blast against murmuring comes in the chapter on fair provision for all, in which
he makes a characteristically clear emphasis upon the different needs of different people. He summarizes this by
expressing the principle:

> Those who do not need as much as some others should
> thank God for the strength they have been given and
> not be sorry for themselves. Those who need more
> should be humble about their weakness and not
> become self-important in enjoying the indulgence
> granted them. (RB 34)

Thus the risk of murmuring is created. Once you treat people
as different, with their own strengths and weaknesses, you
set up a system where visible equality can appear to be
undermined. It is easier in this sense to simply treat
everyone the same, but as we have seen, this runs contrary to
Benedict's awareness of people as individuals.

But there is also an opportunity contained within the practicalities of life. Benedict believes passionately that all
practical activities can and must have a public value. Work

can be a sign of the inner life of a monastery, a sign that can even be reflected in the prices set for monastic produce. So he famously states that:

> In fixing the prices of the products . . . what is asked by the monastery should be somewhat lower than in secular workshops, so that God may be glorified in everything. (RB 57)

Is this not a recipe for financial ruin or unfair competition? The point is simple – Benedict wants the world to look in upon the monastery and say 'This is a house of God', before they even get as far as the church or cloister. He wants this to be visible at the cash register or in the guesthouse. He wants the basic attitude of a monastery to inform even the bottom line. In our world, as in his, that is a sign that people notice.

What happens when things go wrong?

You might think that Benedict's way of running a community sounds a little too good to be true. Perhaps he has forgotten about 'the rebel on two fronts'. What happens, you may ask, when the rebellion gets right out of hand? Is there the monastic equivalent of the foam extinguisher which puts out the fire, and blankets out the problem completely?

We all know, whether Abbot or businessperson, that the leader is challenged to be at his or her best when the going is difficult. It is at that moment the real test comes; what reserves do we have to cope with the unexpected, under pressure? And monasteries have moments of crisis, just as businesses do. At such moments the quality of leadership is tested. But there are lesser crises during ordinary times, when the skill of the Abbot is also put under the spotlight.

The means the Abbot has at his disposal
The monastery is a school, it has a framework of life, it has its own customs and priorities, and its responsibilities. Monasteries have to earn their own living and most engage in some form of active apostolate which brings them into contact with the world outside.

Things can go wrong in any number of ways – individual monks will face crises at one time or another, and part of the Abbot's responsibility is to ensure that his monks are capable of handling these moments. We all know that the most common reaction to a crisis, especially an unexpected one, is to panic. That is precisely the wrong way to get through. Crisis management requires a cool head and clear thinking. More than that, it means that people have to know what their priorities are at that moment, and must trust each other to do the right thing.

The first priority
The first priority in the monastery is the routine of prayer which enables the brethren to focus on the fundamental reason for being a monk. This routine strengthens their commitment to God. Monks get to know their prayers so well – Benedict recommends they say the full 150 Psalms every week – that they can repeat many of them by heart. When the crisis comes, whether the collapse of the community, or persecution, or financial insolvency, or destruction by fire, the monks continue with what they know so well – their prayer. If everything else is under threat, the monk knows that his ability to pray cannot be taken away.

The code of discipline
Benedict expects monks to be 'rebels'. Indeed, he recognized that for the majority, monastic life was going to be a continual struggle against the desires of a rebellious temperament. He

expected strong-minded people to join the monastery, and he foresaw many major rows between the Superior and the 'rebel'. So the Rule gives a number of examples of 'rebellion', a list not too unfamiliar to modern ears: monks can eat too much, drink too much, complain about each other and their Abbot, they can be jealous of their skills, misuse authority, be possessive and misuse the tools of the monastery. They can be slow to get up in the morning, late for meals or prayer, and, most significant of all, they can distance themselves from their Abbot.

This may sound rather shocking, but monastic life is for strong-minded rebels. The monk feels so passionately about the call of God that he moved away from his family. As monks they are still strong-minded, independent and find themselves with others less from friendship than from shared commitment to the ultimate goal.

The process of change may appear to be similar to what happens in any human community: raging emotions, defiance, stomping of feet and slamming of doors. Benedict was aware of this and gave the Abbot clear advice about how to handle it. The perfectionist Abbot would have an impossible time. But Benedict could not legislate against this; he hoped that years of living in community would wear away the perfectionism.

Benedict also allows the Abbot to be flexible, and experience will tell him that whatever arrangements he puts in place, over time, nearly everyone will claim an exception. But when faced with what we might call the 'bloody-minded refusal to co-operate', the Abbot offers the word of scripture, temporary expulsion from community prayer and meals and finally, if none of this works, permanent exclusion from the monastery.

While all this is going on the Abbot looks for signs of repentance and a new determination to wholehearted observance. Once seen, the brother needs to be affirmed and encouraged, rather as the father received back his erring son as told by Jesus in the gospel.

Keeping in touch with the Abbot
Benedict several times mentions the responsibility of each of the brethren for keeping in touch with his Abbot:

> the monk does not conceal from his abbot any sinful thought entering his heart, or any wrongs committed in secret, but confesses them humbly. (RB 7:44)

Then in Lent:

> everyone should make known to the abbot what he intends to do, since it ought to be done with his prayer and approval. (RB 49:8)

Again, when given what he considers an impossible task,

> the monk should choose the appropriate moment and explain patiently to his superior the reasons why he cannot perform the task. (RB 68:2)

Behind these texts lies a much more important commitment by the Abbot to each of his brethren. He must get the right balance between being present at moments of crisis, and not appearing to be on their backs. Each rebel needs space and time to make his conversion to a 'cheerful rebel'. But the Abbot has to be there when he faces a moment of crisis.

The Abbot cannot do this simply by treating every one of his brethren in the same way, for example offering them half an hour's discussion every month. Some will need more and some less. In a large community the Abbot makes sure there are others who can help the brother in need.

On the other hand, no brother should feel that the Abbot is not interested in his work and how he feels: that too is difficult to achieve. It is in this area that an Abbot can have no rules; he relies on the common sense of the brethren and the intuition he is given by God.

11

Customer Relations and Hospitality

Anthony Marett-Crosby
Kit Dollard

'Waiter! Can I have some service please!'

Poor service is all around us. You only have to spend money or ask for a service to recognize how your needs are being ignored. Here are some examples:

- A hospital clinic for outpatients fixes all its appointments for 2 p.m., knowing that the last patient will not be seen until 4 p.m.
- A waitress fails to offer any food with a pot of tea because her shift ends soon and she wants to get away by 4.30 p.m.
- After a three-month wait while the video was on order from the USA, it finally arrived and was found to be a faulty tape.
- A local council insists on providing all residents with a 'wheelie bin' for their rubbish regardless of size of household, age of resident or distance of house from the road. In future collections, it maintained that it would not collect any plastic bags that were not in the bins.

Poor customer care is all about selfishness, indifference to selling and treating everyone the same. Ultimately it is about a fixed, closed mind and a lack of 'wakefulness'.

Here is another example:

A firm of prominent national solicitors, who provided an exclusive service to the top end of the market and had a network of good local offices, decided that it would install a more efficient telephone switchboard in the office. This meant that the receptionist only had to answer the main number while all the executives had their own personal numbers with excellent voicemail facilities. If somebody were out of the office the main switchboard would ring, to be answered by the receptionist who asked if the caller would like to be put through to the voicemail to leave a message. There was no opportunity to leave a message with the receptionist as she had her own workload. After six months the firm realized that it was losing new business enquiries. Investigation revealed that new clients wanted a person to talk to, would not leave personal details on a voicemail and had a feeling of not really being wanted.

As Basil Fawlty said, 'This would be a splendid hotel if it wasn't for the guests!' In achieving good customer relations, priorities are essential and sometimes it needs a complete re-evaluation of work patterns, goals and the mission. In the story above, the firm employed a trained telephone salesperson who was able to convert new clients to business, but more important, after three months was able to develop more business from existing clients.

The key to good customer care

The Halifax Building Society admits that it takes four times as much money to attract new customers as retain existing ones. Many other businesses would claim a higher ratio – in the region of eight to ten. So if customer care is so important, then why is it so bad, and what might the secret be for improvement?

. . . was able to develop more business from existing clients.

In a nutshell, a summary of current customer care strategy in some businesses might look like this:

- First, establish what your customer *really* wants.
- Second, meet that need.
- Third, exceed those needs.
- Fourth, ask for more business.

In addition there are a number of 'given attitudes' from the buyer in almost every case. These might be:

- 'Will you listen to me?'
- 'I am important and my request is valid.'
- 'I am more important than you for this transaction.'

One of the keys to good customer care is a servant-like attitude by the service provider. In response to the request 'Can I have my hamburger with extra tomato sauce, no onion, no gherkin and wholemeal bread?' there are two options – 'Yes' or 'No'. 'No' is frequently much easier, because saying 'Yes' needs a very different attitude. Perhaps it is all about power. In good customer service there is a sense of powerlessness and what it means to put others before oneself completely and utterly – adopting the role of servant. It is only then that the real needs of the customer can be discerned – and exceeded.

The customer ordered salmon and hollandaise sauce, and when asked for a choice of two vegetables declined the greens and just opted for a salad. When the meal arrived there was no sauce. The customer complained. The waiter (who had not taken the order) brought over the order chit, which had the initials 'w/s' against the vegetables. He had interpreted this to mean without sauce, partly on the assumption that he did not like hollandaise sauce – but he had not realized that two vegetables were available that day. The 'w/s' had stood for with salad. So two people were at fault – the waitress for not getting the order down on paper correctly, and the waiter for imposing his preferences on the customer. In the end he was more interested in justifying his own mistake than seeing the customer happy.

Underpromise – overdeliver, remains a key phrase for good customer care: the concept of delighting the customer. Here is an example from the hotel business:

There are two 'travel hotels' in a prosperous provincial town. One is slightly (10 per cent) more expensive than the other. Two executives were doing business close by and needed to stay the night. Both of the hotels had one room spare so they tossed a coin to determine who should have the cheaper accommodation. Ben won and spent a miserable night in the more expensive hotel, which only appeared interested in whether he wanted a cooked breakfast the next morning: and, to make matters worse, the hotel had a sales convention in progress, so that the noise did not die down until the early hours. Ben vowed that he would not go back to that hotel or others in the chain. Mike, who had been in the cheaper accommodation, had spent a most peaceful night and had a cooked breakfast: but what sealed his admiration was the remark by the person at checkout: 'Do you usually keep your credit card receipts of payment with the invoice?' 'Yes,' said Mike. So they were stapled together at the cost of a staple and five seconds – but it made all the difference, at that moment, to customer relations. 'A small touch' said Mike later, 'but she probably knew what our accounts department are like – real sticklers for details!'

Good customer service – or hospitality as Benedict would call it – is an essential element for the survival of any business, from professional services to heavy engineering. What is true of modern business is also true for Benedict's monasteries.

Not only is hospitality a monastic 'growth industry', but it is also among the most powerful signs that a monastery can offer to the world. The principle of Benedictine hospitality is that of the welcome given to all. It was a need of which Benedict himself was acutely aware, and many communities since his day have had cause to smile ruefully at his words in the Rule that 'monasteries are never without guests'.

The basics

Benedict's chapters on guests are informed by two basic considerations. The first is that guests arrive at unpredictable times and do strange and apparently awkward things. So Chapter 53 is not concerned primarily with the kind of guest who announces their arrival three months in advance, knows the community well and is determined to be invisible for the moment of arrival to the time of departure. Such guests are always welcome, but they are also very rare. Benedict's chapter is concerned with 'any guest who happens to arrive', a point which Benedict stresses by laying down specific practices such that:

Guests . . . may not unsettle the community by arriving, as they do, at all times of the day. (RB 53)

This superficial inconvenience is of course a sign of something far deeper. A guest is one who may not share any of the assumptions that underlie the monastic life or even the Christian faith. In all sorts of ways, we lay out tests for the guest, by which they can reveal themselves as being different or unfamiliar, and probably the greatest test of all is how they respond to their first encounter with the monk. As we will see, Benedict has a very specific vision of how that encounter should take place.

The second underlying assumption behind what Benedict has to say concerns not the guests but the one who receives them. It is simply this – the way we welcome a guest reveals more about what is going on inside our community than anything else. This is a most important point of contact between Benedict's treatment of hospitality and the needs of business. What kind of community do we show ourselves to be by the attitudes behind our hospitality?

Benedict is unequivocal in declaring that our attitude to strangers demonstrates the real depth of our Christian commitment. In saying this, he is locating the principle of hospitality in a particular context, the powerful and terrifying parable of the Last Judgement in the Gospel of Matthew. It is the story of the separation of sheep from goats, of God's welcome to those on his right who have fed him when hungry, clothed him when naked and welcomed him when a stranger. In answer to their enquiry, 'When did we see you like this?', God offers the extraordinary statement: 'Whenever you did this to the least of my brethren, you did it to me' (Matthew 25:40). Benedict uses this parable, which reveals what lies at the heart of a Christian vocation, very sparingly. In fact, he applies it to our attitude to just two groups of people, first the sick within the community, and second to guests. The point is obvious – both groups are inevitably going to interrupt our settled routines, our plans for the day. The unexpected arrival and the sick monk in need of help cannot be fitted neatly into our diaries. The challenge of the guest demands of us that we look for the opportunities presented by life beyond the diary. So are we prepared to change the plans we have made for them, or not? Benedict wants a monastery to be a place where there is always room for the one who knocks on the door.

One of the most famous stories that illustrates this approach is told by Bede the Venerable of St Cuthbert. As a young monk, Cuthbert was sent to a new monastery at Ripon, where he was appointed guestmaster. There, we are told, he encountered a young man who had arrived overnight, who was sitting in the guest chamber at the beginning of another busy day. Cuthbert's response to this new arrival was to wash his guest's hands and feet, and to insist that he stay for a meal. All this was a normal encounter between monk and guest, until the young man disappeared, and turned out to have been an angel in disguise. The point of the story is clear enough – you never know who you are welcoming!

So if you do not know who it is that you are welcoming, good customer care becomes very demanding, and perhaps that is one of the primary reasons in business that we do it so badly.

Giving and receiving

When Benedict explores the nature of guests and the reason why they are worth welcoming at all, he identifies the guest as being like Christ. This is not done lightly:

> Those attending them both on arrival and departure
> should show . . . that it is indeed Christ who is received
> and venerated in them. (RB 53)

This is powerful language. Benedict is not talking about a quick smile, a cup of tea and an apology for being too busy to do anything else. He talks about receiving, that is making space for the guest within the established group, and even about venerating him or her. This might almost seem a blasphemy if taken too far! Benedict's response to this fear would be 'Good – take it too far'. There are no half-measures in Benedict's treatment of guests, and the greeting of those who come is not delegated to somebody with nothing better to do. In fact, he urges that:

> As soon as the arrival of a guest is announced the superior and members of the community should hurry to offer a welcome with warm hearted courtesy. (RB 53)

Look at the verbs that Benedict uses. The first is the apparently innocuous 'announced'. But this is important – the guest is not someone who finds himself or herself in the middle of the community only after he has fought his way through a series of barriers. Rather, the arrival of the guest is meant to be a moment when the monks actually *hurry* to do something, almost the only time Benedict uses this kind of language. Third, a welcome is *offered*, in the sense that we might offer someone a present. Again, this is very deliberate, because Benedict sees the interaction between the community and a guest as an exchange of gifts.

Let us look for a moment at what the guest can give. At the very end of his chapter on hospitality, Benedict deals with the awkward practical situation of a monk who encounters a guest during a time of silence. He says that, first, the monk should greet them with the proper respect, not glide past as if the person interrupting their sacred moments should not exist. But this is not enough: the next thing a monk should do is to seek the guest's blessing, prayer, and then the most powerful gesture of all, the washing of the guest's hands by the Abbot, and the washing of the guest's feet by the Abbot and the whole community.

What is going on here? Benedict wants his readers to see a clear parallel between the greeting of the guest and the encounter between Jesus and his disciples in the Last Supper. The point is being made over and over again – the seeing of Christ in the guest creates the opportunity for a real exchange of gifts, and avoids the twin dangers of using guests as an opportunity to show off the riches of the community, and also of seeing guests as the private answer to our personal needs. Both sides have needs, and both have things to share.

This strategy is quite rare in the business world, and many customer/provider relationships never get to this stage of recognizing their different needs. There was once a survey from the brewing industry that asked why customers visited public houses. The overriding response was the character of the publican – not the decoration, the food or even the beer! It is this sharing of needs, on both sides, that always produces a longer-lasting relationship between supplier and customer. It is this that will weather the inevitable variables of the marketplace of economics, distribution or product.

> Gavin is the Managing Director of a small group of corner shops in the North East. 'I always take time to really understand the needs of my suppliers. Yes, of course they are more powerful than us, but I believe in building relationships that will last. It is something that I can do better than the larger chains of supermarkets.'

Surely this is an attitude that each business should seek to achieve.

Using customer service to grow

To establish growth, measurement is needed. In the area of customer service, assessments are the traditional way of doing this through questionnaires, interviews, mystery shopper surveys and the like. In listening very closely to the customer it is possible to identify 'moments of truth' when a high level of service is critical. For example, in employing a divorce lawyer, the average person with marital problems has no way of knowing the lawyer's expertise as against other lawyers – probably referral or recommendation were the key criteria for appointing that particular person in the first place. So when it comes to assessing the lawyer's perform- ance, the client has to rely on their own experiences, and their set of criteria might be:

- Were the letters written on time and with correct spelling?
- Did the lawyers keep me informed in a friendly and 'kind' way?
- How considerate were they of my feelings?
- How confidential were they?
- Did they meet my deadlines?
- Did they charge me for 'extras' like postage, telephone calls?

These criteria may be very far from what the lawyer thought he was being assessed on! They are highly subjective and will differ from client to client, but they can be measured. So it is important for both sides, but particularly the service provider, to recognize that they can learn and grow from the relationship with the client and to define exactly what it is they are providing.

People make decisions to buy a product or service based on favourability (what they *think* about the product) and famil- iarity (what they *know* about the product). When both favourability and familiarity are high, then they will buy. This may be achieved through the traditional marketing methods such as publicity, exhibitions, sales-force operations, advertising, mailshots and the whole range of communication methods. We are unlikely to buy something if we do not know anything about it, nor if we do not regard it as being any good.

Perhaps Benedict sees his instructions on hospitality as a key method for evangelization. Certainly in the business world the optimum position is to take the customer beyond being 'very satisfied' to the position of becoming an advocate. There is one insurance company that funded its growth for many years by asking each satisfied customer for the names of three possible new customers whom they thought would be happy to buy the insurance policy they had just bought. Undoubtedly the best way of getting new customers remains through word of mouth or personal recommendation.

So good customer service in an organization is an outward sign that everything is going well on the inside. Benedict recognized this, and that is why, like businesses, he makes it such an important issue. It is a temperature gauge to the health of an organization.

12

The Abbot Reflects . . .

Anthony and Kit have brought out the two areas where any organization can get it wrong, whether bad management within or incompetence without: both are as important to the monastery as they are to the business. We have to be good at making the monastery function as community, and we have to be good at dealing with those we serve as a monastery. The business likewise has to be efficient in the way it operates as factory or service, and also be able to respond quickly to the needs of its customers. There is an obvious overlap.

In the past this overlap was less obvious: the more enclosed monastery was founded on a simple lifestyle, and all the needs were found within the enclosure. As soon as communities grew this became impractical, they became functioning organizations, in many respects like their commercial equivalents. They produced things, sold them and from the income bought the things they did not have.

Behind this model was a clear distinction between the members of the community and those who worked for the community employed to 'fill the gaps' created by the absence of suitable monks. For many monasteries this has changed dramatically, and has brought a new dimension to their life – the need to work closely with lay people, as partners or colleagues, in education or parish or hospitality. The sense of monastic control, once so important for a work to be called 'monastic', is now considerably reduced.

In this new situation there is more scope for friction. Monastic work now brings the monk into the lay world where he is expected to work to the same professional standards as the lay colleague beside him. This raises the question of what makes a work monastic: the fact that it is undertaken in the shadow of a monastery, whether there are monks working there or not, or the number of monks working within it? The question has important repercussions both for the community's sense of its worth, its control of its own works and its ability to attract young men to the monastic life.

But there are dangers: the work of the monks may be elevated because of the professional demands ahead of their monastic duties, with the result that the balance between monastic obligations and work is upset. For the Abbot, this system also imposes additional challenges. In the enclosed monastery, with plenty of monks, an Abbot could, at least in theory, move someone from job to job, paying more regard for the spiritual needs of the monk than the efficacy of the job. The Rule defends such an approach.

> Blessed are you if you live everything as grace: you will be graced and agreeable to everyone.

The Abbot encourages his monks to see the inspiration of God at work in the lives of all who work alongside them. In this way the narrow boundaries of parochialism are forced back. Courage, goodness and integrity are found in people from all ages, backgrounds, religions and nationalities. They deserve respect, and the monk should set the example. By affirming it, the monk gives encouragement, especially to those who live on the margins of society.

Anthony and Kit have outlined Benedict's teaching about this in the Rule and given an outline of the ups and downs of hospitality in a monastery. Benedict's approach to guests is precisely the one that brings the best out of them. Greet with a blessing, go off to pray and then offer food and accommodation, all to be done by monks skilled at the task. The line is drawn; the visitor who joins the community in prayer, spends time reflecting on what the life is about and enjoys the regular day, will go away enriched.

But, of course, it does not always work like this. Monks do not always behave as they should, and each of us is a victim of our prejudices. This story shows how prejudice can so easily upset working relationships and destroy a community.

Ezekiel is a quiet, talented craftsman, a man of charm, kindness and integrity. He works for an engineering firm which manufactures farm tractors. He is a Jew and in his youth spent time on a Kibbutz in Israel. There he discovered two things; that he loved the land, and he had considerable practical skills. He is a British citizen and has spent most of his life in Britain. After school he trained as an engineer. Now in his late 30s he is married with a young family and has recently been appointed to head a team responsible for the assembly and testing of new tractors.

No one would have known he was Jewish: he did not parade his religion in public and he lived quietly in the neighbouring town. There was nothing to pick him out from the rest of the employees, except of course his name. He was proud of his name; it was something by which he could express his Jewish faith without being too ostentatious. In the years he had worked in the factory it had been a topic of mild fun and he had enjoyed it: nothing very serious, and it allowed him to make friends. He had a sense of humour.

Because he was fair and had high standards, the team worked well and had one of the highest scores for productivity and excellence. He was respected by all. At the same time he was also liked by senior management; he was a man with a future; his colleagues could see him rising to more senior positions; he was offered and took the opportunities the company provided for in-service training.

A change happened when a new group of young engineers was employed. They were dispersed among the teams at the plant, one engineer to Ezekiel's team. It soon became clear he did not share the team's view on certain issues. The new engineer did his work, but he also enjoyed making comments to Ezekiel designed to irritate him. They were personal and focused on his religion. In general discussion this new group stuck together and enjoyed taking political positions, similar to those of the National Front. They were not aggressive, but some employees felt uneasy.

This unease pointed to a crisis in the future if something was not done soon: but it was difficult to know precisely what. The employers could not prevent political discussions.

Nothing inflammatory or really abusive had been said. Ezekiel, though uneasy, was unable to pinpoint the problem.

Then one day an accident occurred: an electric spark blew the main fuse and the works came to a standstill. It was serious enough for an enquiry, but not so serious as to endanger life. It halted production for a few hours. The word spread among the workers that Ezekiel was at fault. The incident happened close to where Ezekiel's team were working, but it was an accident that could have had a number of causes. There was no clear link between Ezekiel's team and the spark, but that did not stop a group of workers going to the Plant Manager with an official complaint. They refused to continue working while Ezekiel was still in charge of a team.

Ezekiel was called in by the Plant Manager, who informed him of what had happened and sent him home for the rest of the day while an investigation was carried out. He was upset by this, but thought it was the best way to allow things to get sorted out. It was Friday afternoon and he would be back on Monday morning.

Once Ezekiel was away, the discontented workers raised their demands: they wanted Ezekiel's immediate removal on the grounds that he was unreliable. The Plant Manager, sensing the situation was fast getting out of hand, called in a senior team of engineers to work over the weekend to find the cause of the electric spark.

Later that same Friday afternoon the discontented workers organized a meeting of all the teams at a local pub. There they put a number of points and said that Ezekiel was the cause of the problem. He was Jewish and he had to be removed instantly; nothing would go right with him there. All were asked to support the motion. In such a heavy atmosphere no one stood up for Ezekiel. The motion was carried and one of the discontents was commissioned to deliver the note over the weekend to the Plant Manager. If Ezekiel was reinstated on Monday the workers would walk out.

The investigation team reported late on Sunday afternoon that the spark was caused by a faulty electrical switch which had been repaired two days previously by in-house electricians. The accident was waiting to happen and had nothing to do with any of the teams working in the factory either at the time of the spark or any other occasion. The case against Ezekiel was unfounded.

Just after the Plant Manager received that report, the resolution of the workers was brought to him.

How should he react?

Such situations put any manager to the test. Quick reactions, sound judgement and an accurate understanding of the people involved are the key to a successful outcome. If the manager knows his workers, he will also know how serious the situation is and whether he can wean them away from this extreme position by personal persuasion.

It also shows the need for continual education: time and investment to ensure all are encouraged to develop positive attitudes towards others. Information about the laws respecting the rights of individuals should be available and opportunities provided for all to understand better the different cultures, religions and behaviour.

There is no doubt that the manager will have to reinstate Ezekiel, but if it is done in the wrong way, it will make the matter worse. This is not a case for using blunt, authoritarian tactics, nor is it a case of giving in to the demands of the minority. To win over the majority of the workers may need a great deal of painstaking work with individuals. Quick action is needed, but time is not on the manager's side.

The monastic guestmaster's misjudgement may cause the Abbot a problem, as this story shows:

Brother Rock has been an outstanding guestmaster of the monastery's 45-bed guesthouse for some ten years. He has increased the bed-occupancy rate and opened the doors of the monastery to a wider group of people. He does not ask much of his guests and has been aware that some have misused the hospitality. But, he says, that is the risk you take if you are to open the door to Christ. Up to this point nothing too bad has happened and the contribution of the guesthouse to the monastery's finances has become increasingly important, because the sales of home-made jam have slumped following a bad summer. A few weeks ago Brother

Rock was approached by a man asking for a room with a double bed for the weekend. The room was booked. The man arrived and collected the keys. Brother Rock sees little of them over the weekend, but the bill is paid and the keys are handed back. He thinks nothing more of it. A fortnight later the Abbot gets a phone call from a friend alerting him to an advert on the Internet: 'Abbey Guesthouse: The honeymoon centre for gay couples'. Brother Rock's name is given as the person to contact.

How would you advise the Abbot?

How can I keep a cool head
in a changing world?

To Live is to Change

Anthony Marett-Crosby
Kit Dollard
Abbot Timothy Wright

Change is dangerous. It has other nasty features as well – it is always stressful and it inevitably creates great fear. Very few of us embrace change willingly. So why does it happen so often? The reality is that unless we change we remain static, and that in the end means death. Every living organism changes and so to live we need to change. 'To live is to change, and to be perfect is to have changed often,' said Cardinal Newman.

This chapter is divided into a look at organizational change followed by individual change. Clearly the two are related, but organizational change with Benedict is largely a matter for the Abbot, while individual change is part of us all. We will look at how Benedict handles change in an organization by how the newcomer is an agent for change and is welcomed into the community.

Changing the organization

There are many writers who have led the way on organizational change – Bennis, Thompson, Drucker, Kanter and Harvey Jones. This is not the place to undertake a review of their thinking; however, a brief summary of the process of change is useful in our conversation with Benedict.

Finney[1] proposes seven elements of change:

1. *Magnitude* – some big changes may need stages.
2. *Speed* – the need to balance new challenges with stability of the group.
3. *Direction* – balancing the U-turn with the completely unknown.
4. *Threat to status* – changing the *status quo*.
5. *Confusion* – a wise leader will see that dissent is seen as welcome.
6. *Misunderstanding* – knowledge gives a sense of control while uncertainty brings fear.
7. *Drive* – ensuring that the positive forces are not cancelled out by the negative.

Higginson[2] says there are five important aspects to managing change – vision, communication, consultation, sensitivity and resilience. Other writers go further and insist on change only being successful when 'change agents' are given the task of facilitating change. In many ways Benedict's Abbots are the change agents of a community.

Research by Rogers and Shoemaker (among others) showed that people accept change at different rates. They distinguished five groups of people:

1. *Innovators* – who like change and often initiate it.
2. *Early Adopters* – the first group to be persuaded.
3. *Early Majority* – the bulk of the people.
4. *Late Majority* – more cautious individuals who are less easily caught up by the movement of support.
5. *Laggards* – unlikely to be persuaded.

Justin Dennison illustrates the way in which an average group responds to change – from the negative attitude of the Laggards to the positive attitude shown by the Early Adopters. Most leaders come to accept that the Laggards will probably vote against *any* change in any situation. For the individual faced with a change situation, there are two options: you either stay or you leave. As we will see, Benedict has other ideas.

Change in the individual

An analysis of the UK population of Myers-Briggs Types,[3] published in 1998, reflects a rather conservative nation of individuals who tend to prefer facts to possibilities, making decisions based on analysis rather than personal values, and a preference for details compared to the 'big picture':

Combination of perception and judgement	*% UK population*
ST (Sensing Thinking)	36.4
SF (Sensing Feeling)	40.1
NF (Intuitive Feeling)	14.0
NT (Intuitive Thinking)	9.5

There is a clear picture here of people who might be described as having their 'feet on the ground' and certainly not prone to change for change's sake. Perhaps that is one of our national characteristics, but the reality is that the business world is forcing change on even the most change-resistant organizations like banks, hospitals or education. That means individuals must change too.

Arthur Bartram, a wonderfully creative thinker, in *Navigating Complexity*[4] gives details of 'mind tools for navigating complexity'. These are aimed at helping people cope and respond to the complexity that is now part of our everyday business lives. These tools include this advice:

- Be a different thinker.
- Think relationships.
- Think network.
- Think community.
- Think pattern management.
- Be a different learner.
- Be a better listener.
- Be a volunteer.
- Be a wider reader.
- Be a post-modern apprentice.

Bartram also talks about the 'area of chaos' as one of the most fruitful places for creative change to occur. His chaos theory has little to do with the management guru Tom Peters, but is described as the place where order makes the transition to complexity and so to creativity, change and growth. Bartram insists that all living organisms operate in the zone of complexity – but that does not mean it is a comfortable place in which to be!

Greater career choice equals opportunity or threat?

Very few of us can get through our business lives without adapting our jobs or ourselves. The patterns of employment have altered radically in the last twenty years and the concept of career portfolios is common, with many executives planning at least four changes of careers. In the USA it is normal to think in terms of six career changes.

'You will need to think of yourself as an intellectual nomad, rooted in knowledge rather than in any one organization – and of the world as your marketplace' is the introductory advice in a book *Employability – Your Way to Career Success* by Susan Bloch and Terence Bates,[5] which seeks to help business people in their careers.

Through technology and education, we now have greater

freedom to shape our working lives. This brings with it almost as many problems as opportunities, and perhaps for those entering the workplace for the first time, the reality of being threatened by the almost never-ending variety of careers. Thirty years ago who had heard of a 'serious' career as an aerobics instructor, protocol software consultant, and therapeutic masseur? Now there are recognized qualifications and career paths for each of these professions. For many job-seekers though, a simple job for life in a simple industry would be their preferred option.

'I have advised my children not to enter a career until they are at least 28. They are spending the time before then networking,' said a retired executive recruitment consultant. 'By this I mean that they are working for about a year in a variety of different industries, financial services, software or education with the idea of seeing it from the inside. They will then have an idea where their gifts lie but more importantly will have a whole raft of different contacts.'

Time will tell whether this brave advice is right. Many advisers say by contrast that the earlier you get in to your first job the better. The truth is that the right course probably lies somewhere between the two, for in the tough competitive world of getting your first job, the young cannot afford to be seen to be on sabbatical for too long. But what happens if you get into the 'wrong' job or industry?

You have to love what you do. Ten years ago, Annoushka Ducas was spending her days driving to the coast at 4 a.m. to buy fish, having taken over the running of her mother's fish business. Today, aged 35, she runs Links of London, a jewellery company with 24 shops and a turnover of £9.4 million. The idea for the business, which started by selling fish cufflinks, was a happy accident. Her mother wanted some gift ideas for her customers, and when some of Annoushka's cufflinks were left over, she tried selling them to Harvey Nichols in her lunch break. Two years later, her husband worked out a business plan and she hasn't looked back. 'You have to love what you do' she advises others. 'If you don't, it's an uphill struggle.'[6]

Benedict has always been in the business of developing human gifts and encouraging followers to love what they do. In the Rule it is usually the Abbot who takes the central role of the mentor, for he must 'manage everything in the monastery so that the strong may have ideals to inspire them and the weak may not be frightened away by excessive demands'. But how does this relate to today's businesses?

Personal development is about continuous change. 'You are only as good as your last job' is a rather dated saying, but it forces us to keep looking over the horizon and not to sit on our laurels. Three times in the Rule's Prologue the follower is encouraged to 'run while you have the light of life'. So Benedict also talks about the image of setting out on a journey, and our newly-begun careers become a journey through a continuously changing landscape: a landscape that needs to be seen, looked at and examined.

The key to developing careers is to plan ahead.

Alexander, an insurance broker aged 32, has changed
careers three times, but is now the CEO of a firm of 300
staff. 'It is not a matter of thinking of the next job, but the
one after that. You cannot afford to be hanging around on
the platform of jobs waiting for the right train to come in.'

Although the emphasis is clearly on individuals planning
their own careers, the whole trend of the last ten years has
forced HR departments and CEOs to pay more than lip-
service to succession planning and maintaining key staff. For
some companies, five years is the longest that managers
should do a particular job. Then it is time for a change up,
down or sideways.

Let us now turn to how Benedict handles the change rep-
resented by a newcomer coming to the monastery.

Not much of a welcome

The first thing that Benedict does may seem slightly strange.
You might have thought that it would be natural for him to
encourage his communities to welcome those who seek to
join. After all, without new life, a monastic community dies
remarkably quickly. But quite in contrast to the model of the
guest, Benedict states:

Do not grant newcomers to the monastic life an easy
entry, but test the spirits to see if they come from God.
(RB 58)

The change of feel between the two approaches could not be
more obvious. Benedict nowhere intimates that the potential
recruit is to be seen as Christ. When dealing with someone
who might never leave, and whose coming will change the

You cannot afford to be hanging around on the platform of jobs waiting for the right train to come in.

shape of the monastery irrevocably, a very different approach is used. Benedict declares:

> If a newcomer goes on knocking at the door and after four or five days has given sufficient evidence of patient endurance and perseverance . . . let him be received in the guest quarters for a few days. (RB 58)

Why the reluctance to even let the aspirant in through the door? It is precisely because of the importance of a new member to the community that Benedict is so cautious. He understands the impact that another person, with all their individual qualities, will make upon those already in the community. It is part of Benedict's instinct to take people seriously that leads him to this caution, and monastic experience has proved him right. The temptation to grab at those who want to join is insidious for any community, because it risks undervaluing or even ignoring the potential that we all have to make a difference. No monastery can accept new recruits on the assumption that they will change nothing – quite the opposite, they will change everything.

Why have you come?

The opening of the front door is only the first step in the path of two-sided discernment that Benedict describes in Chapter 58. I say two-sided with emphasis, because it would be to misunderstand the Rule to imagine that the decision rests solely with the one who wishes to join. So Benedict constructs a system whereby the question 'Why have you come?' is posed not once, but many times. Every three or four months, indeed, Benedict wants the aspirant to be confronted by the demands of the Rule and to be told:

> This is the law under which you ask to serve. If you
> can be faithful to it, enter; if you cannot, then freely
> depart. (RB 58)

From the point of view of the community, this requires
honesty. It is always tempting to hold back some of the less
beautiful details of monastic life, hoping that these will just
'become clear' in some mysterious way, hopefully after the
aspirant has made a positive decision. This runs contrary to
Benedict's instinct to reveal to the one who comes the whole
story, the whole Rule, the community in all its strengths and
weaknesses. He wants the people who live that life to show
themselves as they are, not as theory but as living reality.

From the other side, the aspirant is presented with the
repeated challenge to choose. In Benedict's vision of personal
formation, no one can be allowed to drift into a situation
when choosing to stay is just the easier thing to do. We see
this at work in his treatment of priests who wish to join a
monastery. These are people who have already been through
a process of formation, who have already held office in the
Church. In one sense, you might expect a fast-track into the
community, on the basis of a proper respect for what they
have already learned. But Benedict does the opposite. His
principle is that:

> An ordained priest who asks to be received into the
> monastery should not be accepted too quickly. If
> however he shows real perseverance in his request, he
> must understand that, if accepted, he will be bound to
> observe the full discipline of the Rule and may expect
> no relaxations. (RB 60)

How is this discernment to work? Unusually, Benedict here
prescribes a series of rigid tests, three signs as it were which
can become evident to both sides in the journey of discern-

ment. Fundamentally, the question for any aspirant to a Benedictine community is whether they truly seek God, but in case this can be too vague, too theoretical and not grounded in the sometimes hard reality of monastic life, Benedict cashes this out in terms of questions:

Do they have a real love for the work of God, a willing acceptance of obedience and of trials? (RB 58)

These are not tests at the level of theoretical knowledge, nor can they be brushed aside by the fervour of the new recruit. Benedict acknowledges such enthusiasm, respects it for what it is, but regards it as untrustworthy when facing important decisions. These are tests to do with that quality already mentioned, perseverance. This is what Benedict wants to see, not only in the good times but when times are hard, unrewarding and, above all, monotonous.

All this can be as true of a follower of Benedict as it can be of a new recruit – or someone who will not change (a Laggard) – in business. Somehow we can and must make the effort to use the talents of those who might at first be awkward or appear 'not to fit in' – provided they are competent at their work. It is more than trying to be 'accommodating' because the newcomer might just be the key to the future of the company. It is too easy to accept that our newcomers must be like us, must wear the same clothes, must think like us. Why else did Belbin insist that the most successful teams must include the team role of a Plant?

Before we leave this subject of change, there is one other factor that needs addressing apart from job satisfaction.

The work–life balance

For some years, many have been concerned with the imbalance of work and life. The Department of Education and

Employment (DfEE), Parents at Work, and Employers for Work have all contributed to highlighting the issues. As a result, 'businesses have come to realise that working life is changing and that individuals are often having to juggle a wide range of responsibilities, both at home and at work. Large organisations and small cannot afford to ignore the importance of work–life balance; it brings real benefits, both for the organisation and the individual' (Sally Evans, Lloyds TSB).[7]

The benefits of improving the work–life balance are to be found in many case studies. Here is one:

> Hyder plc, a merged water and electricity utility, is the largest plc based in Wales. The business has invested heavily in training and development and therefore wants to retain staff who are regarded as their best asset. In its call centre it operates twenty different shift patterns, designed to meet the needs of the business and of staff; job sharing is available for staff in advisory and first-line management roles (two team leaders are currently job sharing); all staff have been asked for their shift preferences and the business has been able to accommodate 99 per cent of these; staff are able to swap shifts, and special leave and emergency time off is available. The business benefits have been considerable: staff turnover at the call centre is less than 1 per cent (which is very low for this type of work) and staff are loyal and highly motivated. For instance, on Christmas Day last year, during bad weather and storms, the call centre rang staff on Christmas morning asking whether they could come into work. Every member of staff who was contacted came in.[8]

*   *   *

The Abbot reflects . . .

Kit points to the insecurity in the labour market, but many people still work in the same place for a long time. The young, ambitious executive might be advised to change often to gather wider experience for the next step up the ladder. But many people continue to live in the town in which they were born, or have lived for decades. Old people, especially those in retirement, rarely move unless their health demands it.

The bigger issue we face is the challenge to move out of ourselves and build friendship with others, friendships which force us to change, to commit and to persevere in good times and bad.

Benedict's teaching is important and all Abbots recognize the wisdom of the following:

> If you do not want your audience to go to sleep, be brief; if you want to please, be natural; if you want to bore, try to be encyclopaedic. Do not try to be funny, but if you want to communicate, communicate yourself, be enjoyable and enjoy yourself.

People are more likely to change if they feel there is no threat, the decision is theirs. The role of the Abbot is to meet each of the brethren where they are and not pretend they are somewhere else. At the same time it is important to be relaxed and cheerful, as if nothing said about you is meant personally! Cheerfulness can easily be overdone and become tedious, but to offer it as a leitmotif of daily living helps to remove clouds that might appear. In the monastery there is always something to wonder at because the brethren never cease to surprise, by their intuition, their skill, their incompetence and their stupidity: and they will probably say the same about their Abbot! It all goes to show that people change at different rates. Getting it right is often a miracle.

The same can be said of life outside the cloister; there are so many generous people in factories, offices, schools and hospitals. The fact that they are often unappreciated shows a failure in leadership. Perhaps too much emphasis is put on correct administration instead of relating to people and encouraging their generosity.

One day there must be a revolution: until then we still face the difficulty of admitting new people, of appreciating them, and affirming them. Sad to say, many are abused and become victims of the people they thought were colleagues. This story is precisely a case in point.

Angela is 25 years old, attractive, skilled and efficient. She has been a secretary for three years and is starting to think of promotion to PA. She is unmarried and enjoys a full social life. She has been brought up by loving parents but, as the only child, found it necessary to move away from home, much to her parents' disappointment.

Her first job was with a small company that manufactured tinned foods. She was part of a small team of secretaries servicing the directors. It was a lively office and work was stimulating. Her colleagues were more experienced but accepted her as their favoured daughter; she learned much from them. Many demands were made; she performed well. Her first appraisal identified her talent: she was marked for promotion. As time went by she realized promotion was not going to come quickly in the company. Her colleagues were well trusted and they had plenty of years to serve. Angela was ambitious and decided to seek other jobs.

An advert for a job in a smart property company attracted her. She sent for details and liked what she read: it was a company that emphasized moral standards in all

its dealings. The company specialized in high-value residential property in London and the South East. The job
advertised was PA to the Senior Partner in London. After a
long and gruelling selection process, Angela got the job.

After a few days, she discovered the atmosphere in the
office was far from pleasant. There was thinly disguised
resentment of Angela's presence; she lacked the sophistica-
tion, the accent and dress sense, which would have made
her 'one of them'. They felt she would not be up to the job.
The resentment grew worse when they realized the extent
of her competence and dedication.

Angela got on well with her boss, a particularly
demanding man; she was able to meet his demands, something no previous PA had achieved. She found the other
partners pleasant and appreciative. After some months she
asked her boss if she could find another room, saying the
atmosphere in the shared office was affecting her work. By
chance one of the partners was moving out, and she was
offered the office. Her place was taken by the recently
appointed Director of Human Resources – a young man,
eager to please, charming, well spoken and with good con-
nections. He enjoyed being the only man in the office, and
the others adored him. Angela was glad to be away from it
all.

Though her work continued to be both challenging and
enjoyable, her position was vulnerable; her boss was away
for long periods and she was left alone to look after his
affairs. There was little sense of community; Angela was
lonely.

Quite suddenly, late one Friday afternoon, with her boss
already gone, Angela was working to get everything completed before the weekend. There was a knock on her door
and in came the Director of Human Resources. He wanted

to speak to her, and put on his 'charming' smile. The conversation was his way of inviting a relationship; she rejected his advance, and continued working. He forced her to the ground; she started screaming. He panicked, seized her handbag, rushed out, slammed the door, locked it with her keys and fled. By now the office was empty. Luckily she had her mobile and was able to call the police. An hour later they rescued her. She was in emotional turmoil. They took her to hospital for treatment; after a few hours she was able to return home. The following day she went to the police station to give a statement.

Over the weekend the press got hold of the story and splashed it on the front pages on Monday morning. Angela was signed off work by her doctor and she left a message for her boss. In the office that Monday, the staff were furious; they thought the whole thing had been wildly exaggerated, and they resented the press portrayal of Angela as an innocent martyr. The young man, who had given his account to the police on Sunday, was given a hero's welcome when he came to the office. The company feared the scandal would erode its name. The secretaries demanded Angela be dismissed immediately. Her boss, pressed by the other partners to achieve a clean break, complied, with considerable misgivings. Angela received a letter personally delivered that afternoon saying her contract had ended and a payment was enclosed. It was large enough to tempt her to keep quiet.

What should she do?

Angela has a simple option: she can remain silent, negotiate as high a payment as she can, with the help of a good lawyer, and then seek another job with a good reference. Or she could speak out, take the case to the courts and by this means expose the hypocrisy of the company and their lack of proper care for their employees. Most would go for the quiet route, arguing that further public exposure would not make things any better. Publicity has already occurred; the company know they have a problem to resolve and further exposure would not help them deal with it. But some may encourage the public option on the grounds that compensation could be increased.

This problem highlights an endemic problem in our Western societies – the more powerful a company or person is, the more likely they are to dictate terms and buy off those who are critical. The result is that problems rarely get properly dealt with, and individuals get away with exploitive and abusive behaviour with relative impunity.

Change for the better may be slow. It may be held back by a culture which prefers a divided and exploitive environment, working against the weak and vulnerable.

This case from a monastery offers a further point for reflection.

Brother Rascal was clothed as a novice about six months ago. Prior to that he had spent many weekends in the guesthouse trying to discern his possible monastic vocation, and after much prayer and advice he had applied and been accepted as a postulant. His three months as a postulant passed quickly, Brother Rascal excelling in his punctuality to Office, his readiness to help the elderly brethren, and in the speed he picked up the customs of the monastery. The community was small (under fifteen monks) and most of them were over 65. Brother Rascal was one of five under the age of 40. The lifestyle was rigorous; the monks lived in great simplicity, but the regime was harsh; indeed the abbey had limited resources for any form of treatment. In this monastery even the oldest had to be healthy. But the brethren were delighted that they had recruited such a promising novice and showered praise on Brother Rascal. The Abbot was quick to point out that he was still only a novice, and only midway through his first year. In the middle of winter Brother Rascal took ill, the doctor was called and he asked for a blood test. The result showed that he was HIV positive. What should the Abbot do?

14

Hard Choices

Anthony Marett-Crosby
Kit Dollard
Abbot Timothy Wright

In this chapter we look at the more difficult and testing decisions facing people in business and see what Benedict has to say. We will look at discipline, forgiveness, hiring and firing, and pay.

Whenever monasteries present themselves as places where nothing goes wrong, they are lying. Precisely because Benedict's Rule is not a statement of abstract spiritual principles but a true guide to the way that men and women can live together, the question of what to do when things do go wrong, and what hard choices an Abbot has to make, is something that Benedict does not ignore. We should note, however, that Benedict's hard choices all involve people, not things. When he thinks at the level of the institution, it is simply in terms of reaffirming its basic mission statement, which is *to be a house of God*. Within this, he sees not 'management problems' but a community of individuals with real strengths and also real failings. It is about choices. So how does Benedict handle these dilemmas?

A detached existence

Perhaps the most frequent form of choice to be taken by a Benedictine leader concerns those monks who find themselves leading lives detached from the community. It is something that happens quite quickly – the monk, for whatever reason, develops a pattern of life which leaves him on the edge. The early monastic tradition, which Benedict interpreted, saw various reasons why this might happen – sadness, boredom with the monastic routine, a sense of lack of real purpose and even a false kind of holiness which might suggest that common activities and even other people are barriers in the way of God.

There are parallels here with the world of work where, for example, an employee who has been with the company for a long time may have lost a sense of direction or values. That is why the annual appraisals system, if properly used and implemented, can become such a useful tool in managing people and their careers.

The question that the Rule poses runs like this: what does the leader do with someone who refuses to fit in with the obvious signs of belonging? The particular monastic example of this that Benedict treats at some length concerns someone who arrives late for common activities like prayer and meals. The choices faced by the Abbot are rather harder than suggested by the mere inconvenience of someone who disturbs others. The first choice is to determine what this behaviour means to the monk himself, why he is doing it and what underlies this choice to be semi-independent. Once that is faced comes the next question, what the best response should be.

For Benedict, the only answer lies in an invitation to return to belonging, but this cannot be done simply by warm feelings and nice words. He wants the individual to notice what semi-detached behaviour achieves, namely isolation and separation. Thus, Benedict requires that the latecomer sit in a separate place from the rest of the community, in order to highlight what it is that he is doing. Benedict does not want the issue to be simply brushed aside – he sees in this pattern of behaviour something rather more serious, and he wants the consequences to be made clear to the individual.

The great majority of business mistakes are not legislative matters. For example, a letter from an estate agent: '. . . we have duly notified the vendor of your decision to proceed with this sale', when the situation was that the sale would *not* be proceeded with. A small typing error that might or might not be obvious, but certainly caused havoc, wasted time and energy and ensured a loss of reputation and credibility with a 'buying chain'. Small, seemingly insignificant mistakes like this may not be disciplinary matters, but it would be wrong to sweep them under the carpet as just a typing error. Deep down it may demonstrate a much greater lack of concern, interest and knowledge of the client's situation.

The monk who will not change

There are twelve chapters in the Rule concerned very specifically with dealing with the monk who refuses to change. The tone is struck at the beginning of this section of the Rule, in which Benedict establishes who he is dealing with:

> Individuals in the community who are defiant, disobedient, proud or given to murmuring or in any other way set in opposition to the Holy Rule and contemptuous of traditions of the seniors. (RB 23)

Two questions are posed to the leader when faced with this kind of monk, of which the first is a judgement as to the gravity of the offence committed. Benedict speaks more than once of the 'due proportion' that the Abbot must exercise in matching response to problem – there is no single remedy for everything. Then a second issue emerges, of whether the monk will understand the response from the Superior. Perhaps in the business world you could say 'Are they competent?'

Benedict conceives of some monks who might find verbal warnings simply incomprehensible or meaningless, and for them other approaches are needed. Always, the goal of the response is of course not simply to promote regret, but to effect change. Thus the key chapter on how the leader should respond summarizes many of Benedict's most essential principles of leadership, here applied to the particular issue of hard choices and individuals who refuse to change.

> Every possible care and concern should be shown for those who have been excommunicated by the Abbot, who is himself also to remember that it is not the healthy who need a physician but the sick. Therefore the superior should use every curative skill as a wise doctor does. (RB 27)

One of these skills which Benedict urges on the Abbot is to recognize that he himself may not be the solution. In fact, the monastic tradition suggests that the monk who refuses to change is, in the end, at odds with his own Abbot, for whatever reason. So Benedict encourages the Abbot to look to the skills of others, who may bring counsel but also confirm that there is room in the community even for the one in difficulty. So Benedict speaks of the:

> Need for the reaffirmation of love which everyone in the community must achieve through their prayer. (RB 27)

In business this is the place of the experienced consultant or the retired employee who has the time, wisdom and synergy to quietly put right the wrongs. In many less hierarchical organizations the use of such people has been invaluable. It may also be the place for the coach or mentor used so successfully in professional service firms.

The soft option

Benedict conceives of a third situation where a very hard choice has to be made – and this too sometimes occurs in business. In the course of his discussion of the procedure to be adopted for electing an Abbot, he accepts the possibility that:

> The whole community should conspire to elect one who will consent to their evil way of life. (RB 64)

The situation he has in mind is when a community takes the soft option, electing as their Superior someone they can control. This might be because the individual is simply unsuited to leadership, but more probably what Benedict has in mind is a community who know they can restrain a leader from making change through knowledge of the leader's own past.

It is worth remembering that Benedict knew something of this himself, albeit from the other side. Benedict had been appointed as Abbot to reform a community that had lost its way, and so much were his reforms opposed that the monks tried to poison him. Benedict then left, saying to the community:

> Go and seek a father suitable to your ways. After what has happened, you cannot have me. (*Dialogues of Gregory* 2.3.4)[1]

Benedict's dilemma of the community who chooses someone because they can control him places hard choices on those who recognize this. In particular, Benedict believes that those outside the monastery who know what the monks are doing, have an obligation to call for help from those with the power to act. The question is: how do they judge? The only way of making this decision for Benedict is to go back to the fundamental mission or purpose of the monastery, which is not to provide a refuge for individuals but to be a household of God. Faced with an institution that is stuck in its own self-interest, Benedict invites those around to pose themselves the question – what is it really for?

In the same way, in business this situation can be seen to justify the power of major shareholders exerting influence on policy or decisions of a company. Perhaps if more 'outsiders' exerted influence on institutions there would be fewer mistakes?

Is there a place for forgiveness in business?

Whenever people live together, there has to be some mechanism for saying sorry, for asking and receiving forgiveness. This has been a fundamental instinct of monastic life from its earliest years, and long before Benedict it was recognized as essential that monks seek forgiveness of God, and also learn how to forgive each other.

A brother committed a fault. A council was called to which the monk Moses was invited. He took a leaking jug, filled it with water and carried it with him. The others said to him, 'What is this, Father?' He said to them, 'My sins run out behind me and I do not see them, and today I am coming to judge the errors of another.' When they heard that, they said no more to the brother but forgave him.

This story, from a collection of tales told of the very earliest monks in the Egyptian desert, demonstrates how forgiveness was linked from the beginning with self-understanding. It shows the need for a community to find some way of forgiving, which in this story starts with the monks' awareness that they themselves need forgiveness. Saying sorry in business can be more difficult.

James was 19 and had been driving for six months. It was then that he had his first car crash. As he stood in the middle of the road with a steaming radiator and water over the road his father's words came back to haunt him: 'Whatever you do, never admit that you are in the wrong.'

The fact is that in the Western world we live a culture of not admitting guilt, even when we are in the wrong. This is compounded by a culture of blame, which encourages individuals and organizations to find somebody to blame when things go wrong. It can be seen in some advertisements on the back of buses, which read 'Injured at work? We can help you get compensation. Ring us. No money, no fee.' What has anybody got to lose? It encourages the delegation of responsibility to others for my faults. In the end it fosters a climate of fear because no one can be honest.

So is there a place for forgiveness in business and, if so, when? This is really the wrong question because most people would answer 'Of course there should – resentment and lack of forgiveness only lay up more problems for the future; but with human nature being what it is, the difficulty lies in the practice of forgiveness, and in the world of work, with all its pressures, forgiveness may be seen as a sign of weakness and we just cannot allow that.' So, if forgiveness in work is the ideal, then how can we make it easier for it to be practised?

The need for forgiveness is one of the invisible supports for the whole journey that Benedict takes in his Rule. There is no chapter that deals specifically with the subject – it is so basic to the monastic instinct that it appears everywhere. Thus every morning, Benedict urges his monks to pay special

In the end it fosters a climate of fear because no one can be honest.

attention to the petition in the 'Our Father' for forgiveness 'because thorns of contention are likely to spring up' (Chapter 13). This is being done, remember, in the context of the monastic choir – if there is need for forgiveness at a time of prayer, we may safely assume that it extends to every other moment when we interact with one another.

In the particular context of a community, Benedict also recognizes the need for what we might term 'mutual forgiveness'. Benedict establishes a forum wherein a monk might spontaneously admit to being at fault, and seek the pardon not merely of the Abbot, nor of the monk who he might have wronged, but of the community as a whole:

> He must at once come before the Abbot and community
> of his own accord and admit his fault. (RB 46)

Maybe this concept of community forgiveness is too challenging in today's business world, so how could we relate it to practical events? Perhaps the starting-point for most companies would be to look at how they got into this muddle in the first place. This does not mean automatically apportioning blame or starting witch-hunts – but it does mean an honest appraisal of the wrongs of the situation.

This has several advantages. First, it treats the employees as adults in the learning situation, and most adults learn by experience. As they used to say in the army, ' You can make as many mistakes as you like – but only make them once.' Second, it encourages an atmosphere of trust, respect and loyalty, ultimately about empowerment. Third, and perhaps most important for the organization and the leader, it forces a review of present operating systems, which can only lead to continuous improvement. Of course there will never be a system, safeguard or procedure to stop all the mistakes in the business world, but the process of continuous review is an essential element of the feedback loop and, when practised consistently, must lead to better products, services and ultimately profitability. Perhaps equally important is that it stops stability or stagnation and encourages change – and therefore life.

'You are fired!'

Ultimately, of course, the Abbot must face the question of whether there can be room for the monk who becomes proud of his refusal to change. Benedict acknowledges that at times the good of the community must lead to the dismissal of the individual – it is the final skill of the doctor to know when to operate, to remove the diseased part for the sake of the whole.

This expulsion is not simply a one-sided judgement. Yes, the good of the community must be preserved, but in making this hardest of choices, Benedict's Abbot should also have the interests of the monk himself at heart. It may be that only expulsion, real separation, will bring about the change of heart that is called for. Thus, the chapter immediately after the one on dismissal concerns the re-admission of those who leave. Restoration into the community is permitted not just once but as many as three times – the hope that the individual will in the end change is thus kept alive for as long as possible.

Here is a story about the dangers of bad HR practice in a small industry.

Ten years ago a small company which manufactures specialist computer processing equipment employed 50 people. A number of small but serious mistakes kept being made in the manufacturing department. Customers began to complain but remained loyal as there were few suppliers in the industry. After investigation the CEO determined to put matters right and fired five employees from the department. He did it in a most aggressive manner and although he followed all the right procedures, managed to build up significant resentment among the five (most of whom were not competent to do their jobs). The morale of the rest of the workforce began to be affected and fear became the driving force behind the leadership style.

The five employees all found work relatively quickly in a competitor company which paid well and was more committed to training and development than its rivals. In time, two of the ex-employees rose to be directors. It was no coincidence that they never did business with their past employer and word spread throughout the industry that the old firm was 'not a nice place in which to work'. As a result, they lost market share and customers. When the opportunity arose for the ex-employees to buy their old firm, they did so, without any malice; but, as one of them said, 'Finding the maturity to forgive the old firm was the hardest thing about this deal.'

So whose fault was this episode? Benedict is clear that 'the Superior manages everything so prudently that the work of the community may be accomplished and whatever duties the community undertakes being carried out without any excuse for murmuring'. In other words, it is the Superior's fault that the mistake happened in the first place: the buck stops with the leader. This is another occasion for wise and courageous leadership.

A final word about money

One final hard choice we might consider, and that concerns money.

Richard was 31 and worked for a software company which he and his friends had started eight years ago. The company had done well and was now worth over £300 million. He had just taken on the job of CEO, had a 15 per cent equity stake and next year would be paid a basic salary of £1 million, with a profit-related bonus. He already had all the money he needed and certainly more than he had dreamed of as a student, but he felt that something was missing. 'Money', he reflected: 'How much is enough?'

This is one of the hardest choices facing businesses. Money is what makes the business go round, it is after all the bottom line, but how much do you *need* to pay people? How much do *they* need? When do you say 'Stop', both as an individual and as a leader? Market indicators and ratios can help – for example, in the residential property world, estate agents used to be paid three times the income they generated for their firm. But for many working in business there remains the difficult question of just where to draw the line.

Of course there are checks and balances in the market economy, and the supporter of capitalism will point to the benefits of wealth creation; but the question remains, 'When does money become unreasonable profit?'

Lee Iacocca writes, 'My father said, "Be careful about money. When you have five thousand, you will want ten. When you have ten you will want twenty." He was right. No matter what you have, it is never enough.' The millionaire John D. Rockfeller was asked, 'How much money does it take to satisfy a man completely?' He replied, 'It takes a little more than he has.'

This is a difficult area for Benedict. He does not talk about the specific issue of money except in the way of possessions and charging for the services of the monastery. His 'reasonableness' seems to shine through in the philosophy of 'You can have what you need' – but there is also a clear responsibility to use money in a constructive way. Benedict's thinking is about stewardship rather than squandering, about responsibility rather than waste. His question would probably be

'Are you using your talents for earning money for the good of all – or just yourself?' In today's world he might even ask, 'Are you a cenobite or a sarabaite?' Are you able to live in harmony with others or is 'your law to do what *you* want to do?'

Living in relationship with others at work is hard. There are difficult choices to be made. Wisdom is difficult to tie down. We all know it when we see it, but it is almost impossible to teach. The Rule refers to 'the wise being recognised in words that are few', which is not a lot of help when the CEO is asked an embarrassing question about a tricky company situation! Wisdom comes from looking back at the past, from learning from mistakes and from accepting that change can only be managed but not resisted. Wisdom is ultimately what Benedict has to offer to the world of today.

*   *   *

The Abbot reflects . . .

> If the miseries of your neighbour arouse your impatience and not your mercy, it is a sign that you have not yet accepted your own.

That is a thought-provoking remark. So often I am irritated by the failings of the brethren; why can't he be on time, just once in the week; why can't he get to bed early enough to be down for morning prayer. I suspect all of us in authority, wherever or whatever, find we say the same thing, at least occasionally.

That is not the right platform from which to correct another. As soon as mistakes or failures become personal for the boss, then that is not the moment to start the process, for we are bound to get it wrong and create a worse situation, enlivened with resentment and anger and frustration on both sides.

But how can one get to that spirit of detachment which enables the proper process of correction and forgiveness to take place? Somehow we have to show that the matter is serious without it being a personal affront – show that the problem lies not with the management but with the individual. Over-reaction tells the offender the management has a problem.

By standing back, keeping things in perspective and adopting an attitude of sadness rather than anger, of disappointment rather than frustration, the offender will come to see where the problem truly lies. Kit speaks of businesses examining their systems and, indeed, that might be needed; more important is to look at the pressures the managers are under and see what can be done to reduce them.

Part of the problem is having the right people in place to achieve this. Holding responsibility for others is demanding, and the pressures, especially when they come on top of a heavy workload, can be so great it is impossible to keep a sense of perspective.

But there is another dimension: if the manager really likes people, likes working alongside people and takes an interest in them as individuals, the problems are never going to be so great. This leads to interest in colleagues which builds trust and support.

There is another step; if we are really to like others, we have to appreciate ourselves. If we are aware and accepting of our weaknesses, we feel less threatened by the weaknesses of others. To be comfortable with our failures is a sure sign we can be comfortable with the failures of our colleagues or brethren. Here again we start by accepting ourselves as we are; unrealistic ambition has to be extinguished, expectations should never be too high and we must be able to laugh at ourselves. With such self-assurance a secure foundation for gaining respect is in place. But even then it can be betrayed, as this story shows.

Antonio is a bright young man of Italian descent. He is in partnership with two others, running a business providing homes for elderly people.

He first qualified as a medical doctor and then decided not to pursue the career. He enjoyed the training, but wanted a life which was more exciting, with more independence. He wanted the easy life; that meant making money.

To get further qualifications he did a part-time course in business studies. With his medical training this provided him with the skills to seek a job in a company working in health care. He joined one of the largest. After a few months, the acute shortage of places for elderly people made him realize there was room for him to found his own company. But he lacked both experience and finance.

He was so highly thought of by the senior management that he was put on the fast track for promotion. He was an expert in finding locations for new homes. During this time he met Jeremy and Emma at a conference for young professionals wanting to set up their own business. Jeremy, an expert in marketing, was Managing Director of a large time-share company. Emma was an accountant. After qualifying in a large city company, she wanted to work in a small company in which she was able to make a more direct contribution to people's lives. All three were of the same age and unmarried.

At the conference they found themselves talking after dinner one night and somehow it all came together quickly: they 'clicked' as a trio. By the following morning they were planning the next steps, to find the capital, undertake the market research, and seek the necessary permissions. It was decided that Jeremy would be the Chief Executive, Emma the Financial Director and Antonio the Development Director.

It took six months to set up the company and establish the first homes. Three years later the company was running 45 homes, mainly in southern Britain, and the business was moving into profit. Their backers were pleased. They decided to spend the next eighteen months consolidating their position.

Later Antonio started to feel unhappy about this decision. He knew there was no point in arguing the case for further expansion, the others had been adamant; stability was needed to make sure all the homes were operating well; they wanted to secure a sense of family in all the homes. With 45 they could achieve this. Their aim was quality, and that meant being small enough to give time to each home. Jeremy, from his past experience, knew how easy it was for companies to become impersonal and lose the edge; Emma was sure that size would threaten that special quality she wanted the homes to have. Antonio was less committed to this. He felt they had found a winning formula, and wanted to capitalize on it with more homes.

A friend offered him the opportunity to be a partner in a business taking over a further ten homes which needed investment as the managing company was going out of business. But to do this he needed money. He knew that he could persuade potential lenders by the using the name of his own company as the guarantor. He was helped because the new homes were in Scotland and the investors would be Scottish. The name of his existing company was well known and his position within it enabled him to use it without questions being asked. He concealed it from Jeremy and Emma.

As time went by he needed more money for the enterprise and so, by a series of carefully planned ruses, he persuaded Emma to lend him money, for 'development' costs. Soon the sum reached £5 million and Emma was getting worried. She advised Jeremy that something odd was happening and they decided to have a meeting, the three of them, to confront Antonio with the problem and ask for an explanation. At the meeting all came to light, as Antonio thought that honesty was the best form of defence.

It was clear:

1. that he disobeyed an agreement between the three of them;
2. that he had used the company's name to further his own business interests;
3. that he had deceived Emma about the money he had asked from her;
4. that he had used the company's money to develop his own business, without a proper agreement;
5. that he had broken trust and put the partnership at risk. More important, he was guilty of a criminal offence.

How would you advise Emma and Jeremy to deal with Antonio?

So much depends on the relationship that has been built over the years. They might have suspected that something was up for several weeks but not taken the difficult decision to confront Antonio with it for fear of upsetting the business. On the other hand, they might have been such friends that they half-expected something like this would happen, knowing his ambitions. In that case they may be able to strengthen their friendship through this betrayal. If the relationship has been truly betrayed, which perhaps is the most likely, then they will need to find a replacement for Antonio, but achieved in an amicable way. A worse situation would arise if all three, in different ways, became so angry that they each fell out with the others. Only the vulnerability of each has contributed to the disintegration. In a poisoned atmosphere, negotiations will be difficult. The lawyers will gain.

This story from a monastery offers another case of deceit.

Father Barka had been a monk for some 45 years, and had quite a following both among his brethren and among lay people as an effective pastor and spiritual guide. He was entirely orthodox in his teaching, and prayerful in his personal life. But he did like doing things his way. He had served on a parish near the monastery for nearly fifteen years and enjoyed contact with people. Congregations had risen during his time, and he had renovated his church with money raised by the parish. In many ways he was an excellent parish priest.

The Abbot was somewhat surprised to receive a letter from a parishioner saying that she wanted to appraise him of certain features of Father Barka's life, features that she felt he should both be aware of and correct. Rather than put it all on paper, she would like to meet the Abbot for lunch at a nearby restaurant, outside the parish and far from the abbey. She insisted he should come alone and not inform Father Barka of the interview. After some thought, the Abbot accepted the invitation and the conditions. He arrived at the agreed place and over lunch she outlined a story of what can only be called systematic verbal abuse of the housekeeper. The complainant had witnessed it on a number of occasions; but knew the housekeeper to be too frightened to say anything about it. The complainant had come to the Abbot because she had witnessed it for the tenth time in five years only last Sunday. During lunch, which Father Barka always took on his own, he systematically criticized and ridiculed the housekeeper. She, the complainant, had managed to tape part of it for the Abbot to hear. It was most upsetting, revealing Father Barka's own personal insecurity. The Abbot was alarmed that this monk and priest, held in such high regard by so many people, could behave in such an insensitive and brutal way towards one of God's vulnerable people.

What advice would you offer him ?

15

Inner Change

Anthony Marett-Crosby
Abbot Timothy Wright

The outer tension that exists in all organizations between stability and change is only the visible sign of the same inner tension within each of us. At the end of this book, we want to explore that inner challenge to change by looking at the three monastic 'vows'. They form an anchor when things go wrong and provide an opportunity for thanksgiving and growth when things go well. In this sense, monastic vows should be seen very much like marriage vows, 'for richer, for poorer'.

So what are these vows? They are *stability*, *conversion of life* and *obedience*. These are really three ways of saying the same thing, three different phrases to describe the promise by the monk to live the Benedictine life to the full. So they refer to one way of life considered under three aspects. The first for Benedict was stability, with which he challenges his newcomers after just two months in the monastery. The second was obedience, the demands of which were placed before the novice after six months. Finally, at the end of the one-year period of discernment envisaged by Benedict, came the promise of conversion of life, which alongside stability and obedience covers every aspect of the calling to seek God in the monastery.

Stability

In many ways, the concept of stability is the root vow for monastic identity. It contains two distinct elements, the first of which is commitment. A monk is committed not to an institution, nor to an ideal, nor to a philosophy or even to the Rule itself. The monk is committed to a community, to a group of people with its own particular past and present and future. Very often, this group of people is tied to a particular place, but it need not be so. Monks have always moved around, and no monastery can ever afford to put its physical location before its community. So what stability does is anchor the monk within a community, for better or for worse.

When John joined the community, the first task he faced was one he had not expected. The Abbot told him that he would have to find a new name, which would become his monastic name. This initially seemed rather strange. John had, after all, become rather used to being called by his name, which was a good Christian name with one of the best patron saints of all. So he started to look for alternatives, leafing through a dictionary of Saints and coming up with all sorts of names, none of which he would ever dream of being called himself. He did not see himself as an Innocent or a Pius, and the thought of being called Brother Sexwulf, a perfectly respectable name in Anglo-Saxon England, filled him with horror. So he asked one of the older monks how he should make the choice, which saint he should choose. He replied in an unexpected way: 'Don't choose your new name just by a saint. Saints are important, but so is the past of this community. Choose a name that has been used here before, so that you take up that bit of our past, of our history and identity.' So John listened to stories that were told about the monks of old, and eventually decided to take the name Austin. It was hardly an original name, and he had to do some work to find out about Brother Austin. But it was a name known and loved in the community and when he told the Abbot, that Abbot smiled. 'Brother Austin was a great man, let us hope that you will share something of his spirit.'

This belonging to a past and a present is an important part of monastic stability, and it provides the context for looking to the future. The promise of stability is not made on condition that certain things change, or that certain works or customs remain in place. That is why stability can never be tied to a particular location, or a particular work of the community. It is a promise to a group of people, with all their faults and failings, that you want to seek God with them.

The second part of the promise of stability is perseverance. Benedict makes this point very clear when he says that what he wants from his newcomers is that they:

Show promise of remaining faithful in stability. (RB 58)

It has rightly been said that 'a monk's charism is fidelity'. This in itself cuts in two directions, since it concerns how we appear and what goes on deep inside us. Perseverance has an external aspect, to do with how we speak and how we support each other. But it also is something that goes to our heart, for there are many ways of appearing stable on the outside while being miles away from stability within. This is not about never daydreaming or imagining that the grass may be greener somewhere else . But it is about not putting those dreams into effect, not making important changes of life because change is in the end more interesting than staying still. There is a vital role for change in the monastic life, but it is not an automatic good.

Obedience

The vow of obedience is the one that seems at first to be obvious. It is also the vow on which Benedict writes most, devoting a whole chapter to the subject towards the beginning of his Rule. He talks of obedience as the way in which monks imitate Christ, such that:

> A soon as a superior gives them an order it is as though as it came from God himself and they cannot endure any delay in carrying out what they have been told to do. (RB 5)

So obedience involves accepting that what we want for ourselves cannot be the basis for enabling a group to live and work together successfully. In the chapter on the forum for monks and Abbots to come together to listen to each other, Benedict warns against 'an obstinate defence of their own convictions' on anyone's part, because that kind of relentless pursuit of an opinion cannot, in the end, be good for others.

Perhaps it is because obedience is so strongly about how to live with others that Benedict coins a phrase which has rightly become famous, 'mutual obedience'. One of the last chapters of the Rule returns to the theme of obedience:

> Obedience is of such value that it should be shown not only to the superior but all members of the community should be obedient to each other. (RB 71)

This concept represents one of his most distinctive contributions to the formation of true community. The call to obedience is not a self-enclosed path of virtue, a narrow

concept of 'me, my Abbot and my God'. It is an open vision of
the possibilities inherent in others, which throughout this
book we have seen is the only true basis of a community. The
good zeal that monks are meant to show lies in this willingness to be open to each other, to listen to what the other
person has to say. This is not a view based on naïve ignorance;
far from it:

> They try to be the first to show respect to one another
> with the greatest patience in tolerating weaknesses of
> body or character . . . so that no one in the monastery
> aims at personal advantage but is rather concerned
> for the good of others. (RB 72)

Conversion and change

Neither stability nor obedience could make sense without the
third promise, that of conversion of life. It is always a danger
that religious vows become static, that they describe things
that either are, or more realistically are not. The call to conversion of life is in effect a vow to change, to never remain
still either in self-satisfied fulfilment or in self-denying
despair. There is no room for the person who thinks they have
got it all sorted out, nor for the temptation in so many to
believe that we will never even get started. It is a vow to
believe in the possibility of change in ourselves, and also in
others.

This necessarily involves that difficult Benedictine concept
of humility, which we have mentioned in earlier chapters. If
you want to find out what Benedict means by change, then
you need to look at the twelve 'steps of humility' that he
describes in Chapter 7. One of the points of his approach is
that the order of the twelve steps makes it impossible to
follow. Benedict starts with difficult areas of personal
change, and then goes on to much easier and apparently less

important things like the frequency with which one is reduced to laughter. His point is that the process of change must cover everything, that nothing is immune from the challenge of moving forward – except a commitment to do so alongside others and not despite them.

The vow of conversion is also about today. In the Psalm that is sung at the beginning of every monastic day, we pray the words:

> O that today you would listen to his voice, harden not your hearts. (Psalm 94)

This Psalm expresses the special and unique quality of today, and the opportunity it contains. It is so easy to delay personal change to a time when one feels less sick, or less tired, or less fat, or whatever it is. We might decide that change in our group is impossible until a certain person is removed, whom we judge to be the problem. All of these are delaying tactics, whereas Benedict wants us to take a vow that challenges us to see this very day, with all its problems, as the forum for moving forward in our own lives for the sake of others. That is in the end the model for Benedictine growth, which is never introspective or self-loving but always involves an invitation to turn more towards God and to the people with whom we are called to live. At the beginning of the prologue to the Rule, Benedict says:

> It is to find workers in his cause that God calls out to all peoples. (Pro 14)

This call is the beginning of our journey of change, and the Rule is a tool to renew our experience of what matters, how we can change towards what is more important alongside others and not against them. So Benedict's prayer at the end of the Rule is:

They should value nothing whatever above Christ himself and may he bring us all together to everlasting life. (RB 72)

*   *   *

The Abbot reflects . . .

I hope you think Anthony's account of the vows a monk takes accords in many respects with the framework that every one of us needs, monk or lay person.

We all have a duty to be loyal to our family, to those living alongside us and to our colleagues at work That shows the relevance of stability. Instability in any or all of these areas brings vulnerability and fear. Many suffer the consequences of social, political or economic revolutionary change and upheaval.

Within any human community, whatever the size, there has to be order, order which is generally accepted and acknowledged. We might call this the obedience of daily living. Disobedience in our communities blurs the line between right and wrong, brings uncertainty and makes people vulnerable.

The longer we live closely alongside each other in family, neighbourhood or work, we realize how important it is to be flexible. We cannot be a member of a community and not then respond to people as their need requires; we cannot be a supportive member of our family unless we are prepared to go out of our way to provide for those in special need; we cannot stay in the same job for years without appreciating the need for us to be open to change. This flexibility is another way of describing the inner freedom which lies at the heart of the Benedictine's vow of conversion.

So when we come to the need for inner change, the worlds of the monastery and business may appear very different when viewed from the outside, but we can perceive a similar

process going on within each. Business without such structures produces crooks and it is good to remember that saying
about the monk: 'the habit does not make the monk'!

We can also recognize the truth of this saying: 'The great
majority of present problems were born in the past. If you are
overly permissive in order to avoid getting into problems, you
pile up problems. A small dose of preventative medicine can
save you many plagues and incurable diseases.'

As Benedict says, the monastery is a school for training
people to serve the Lord better. We can also say business is a
school to train people to look beyond their own future towards
a vision of work which empowers. To achieve this there has to
be some discipline, but its aim is to focus attention on the
future. In the monastery, as in business, leniency by management may bring short-term popularity: but it will ultimately
lead to serious problems, which may be incurable. That is a
frightening thought; the Abbot, especially, has to remember
his accountability.

In the course of this book we have constantly returned to
Benedict's vision – success is founded on a strong community
in which each person counts.

For the manager, as for the Abbot, the responsibility must
not oppress him. He should note the following: 'Blessed are
you if you reflect before you act and laugh before you reflect;
you will avoid doing many stupid things.' Laughter, as we
have said, is the best way of keeping things in perspective. In
our laughter we see ourselves as we are; we cannot be anyone
else.

If we have been used to making decisions in business, then
we hope to look back and notice how we have grown in
wisdom; we have gained that special insight which comes
with experience. So let me offer this thought, as the next
decision beckons. Let us pause and reflect again on the consequences this decision will have on the people involved.
Experience may alert us to the fallibility of certainty. We

cannot predict the future with any accuracy, for good or ill. As we do this we reflect, perhaps a little ruefully, that life would have been so much easier for all involved if we were able to foresee the consequences with greater accuracy.

We all share this experience, and we should not allow it to depress us. We can reflect that it is an essential part of what might be called the 'compelling mystery' of decision-making. Some of us will enjoy the power of the adrenalin in our veins as we prepare to take such decisions. At the same time we reflect on fragility of the base on which we make these decisions. Standing back and looking at others in our position, we recognize the importance of charisma to enable us to carry others with us, which is at its best when linked to the humility which recognizes the fragility of such decisions.

If we place ourselves twenty years forward and try to imagine how our decision has turned out, we notice three things. First, the excitement of the moment has receded to a vague memory; second, the results incriminate or confirm our judgement; third, developments, unplanned and unexpected, but nevertheless real and important. These put planned results, good or bad, into a different perspective.

In that moment we see how relative our decisions are; time and space put them into perspective, down-sizing them so that we have a better idea of our own importance. Then we see how wrong it is to take our plans too seriously and we laugh at our supposed self-importance. Inspired by such a view we can take the entirely healthy view of any decision we take: I hope it does not do too much damage!

Whether we speak of the effect of time, or the forces of history, we see our making of decisions will almost certainly bring about results we did not intend; some, fortunately, will be for the better; others, sadly, will be for the worse and we have to bear the responsibility. In either case, there is little we can do to change things. But to laugh at the scale of our presumption is one way of gaining forgiveness if we should need it.

At this point we return to Benedict. He demands of all monks the ability to listen with the ear of the heart. To listen in this way, we must unblock our ears of the convictions of a lifetime and remain open to the wisdom surrounding us. Our decision-making becomes ever more sure because by looking back we have seen our follies, learned from experience and maintained our self-deprecating sense of humour. We see, now, how true is the saying: 'Blessed are you if you reflect before you act and laugh before you reflect; you will avoid doing many stupid things.'

By letting ourselves be truly what we are, human beings, existing before all else to love and care for each other, we can take heart from St Benedict's advice to the Abbot: 'drawing on discretion the mother of virtues, he must so arrange everything that the strong have something to yearn for and the weak nothing to run from'.

Where has our conversation arrived?

16

Farewells

Can you now do business with Benedict?

> In the future, success will depend on a stable workforce
> of people who can adapt to rapid change. That's because
> no matter what else shifts in the market, relationship
> continuity is increasingly going to be what matters to
> customers, to suppliers, and to investors. Even in a fast
> economy, it's still longevity that counts.[1]

Perhaps this quotation from the American writer Robert
Herman says it all. Benedict wrote his Rule on the cusp of
chaos. The Roman Empire had collapsed and everywhere
there was disorder. Some commentators would say that is
like today. He was inspired by the desert mystics who by
working, living and praying together had devised a way of
living by balancing principle and detailed regulation, and it
was this that formed the basis for his Rule. Since 530 the
detailed regulations have varied, but the principles have
remained the same. Benedict's way has allowed the best to be
preserved as a guide for living, but always been open to new
cultures. That is why it has survived and why it still provides
such a powerful source of wisdom for today.

The Rule offers a framework and a vision for living. It is

like the garden lattice up which we can grow. It provides wisdom and relevance for the next 1,500 years because it is about relationships between people and, in the end, that is what business and Benedict have in common. Without this shared vision there is little to talk about – little conversation. It becomes small talk.

Many things have not been mentioned in this book; we want to present one single message, which can be summarized in this sentence:

> When man does not recognise in himself and in others the value and grandeur of the human person, he effectively deprives himself of the possibility of benefiting from his humanity and of entering into that relationship of solidarity and communion with others.

This book has unashamedly been people-orientated. We are proud of that because Benedict was very orientated towards the individual rather than the task.

We hope that we have affirmed your past, challenged what you are doing today and given inspiration for the future. Life with Benedict, as in business, is always an adventure, the results are never guaranteed and it usually involves risk.

The darkened auditorium was packed with over 500 business leaders. It was one of those big management conferences and the speaker was drawing to a close. Centre stage, on the dais, was a pyramid of empty drink cans. 'We are now going to try a unique experiment' he announced, 'I want you all to concentrate with all your energy for one minute on knocking over these cans.' 500 pairs of eyes and brains went to work. At the end of the minute, the speaker strode on to the stage and knocked over the cans with his hand. 'The lesson, ladies and gentlemen, is that you can sit and think about something all your life, but if you want it to happen, you have to do something!'

Benedict would surely have laughed at that. In the Prologue there is a sense of urgency that commands action. 'Let us rouse ourselves from lethargy . . . ', 'Run, while you have the light of life . . . ', ' . . . we must hurry forward . . . ' Here are calls to action, to do something, to make a change. But as we have seen with Benedict, it is not just random change but change that is anchored in stability and obedience.

What changes might Benedict ask us to think about in our businesses? Here are some points for your reflection and then for decision:

- How seriously do we take our mission statements?
- How can we really put people first in our businesses and demonstrate this to our customers?
- How do we handle 'the weak'?
- Are we listening to the wise and the 'young'?
- How much are we adapting our leadership styles?
- How fulfilled am I in my working life?
- Is there a place for forgiveness in our businesses?

So, if there is one thing you would take away as a result of our conversation, what would it be? Tomorrow, what will you do differently at work? And perhaps more difficult – what will stop you achieving it? It is sometimes only in the naming of the obstacles in our life that we can win through.

We have reached the end of our conversation.

Let us leave the last word to Benedict, who frequently repeats himself! Chapters 4 and 19 include the phrase 'God is present everywhere . . . '

. . . God is present everywhere.

Notes

Chapter 1
1. All extracts from Benedict's Rules are taken from *Saint Benedict's Rule* by Patrick Barry OSB (Ampleforth Abbey Press, 1997).

Chapter 2
1. For an introduction to Investors in People see www.investorsinpeople.co.uk
2. *Regula Magistri*, eds A. De Vogue and J. M. Clement (Paris: Sources Chrétiennes, 1964–5).
3. Leo Burnett, Chairman, Leo Burnett advertising agency.

Chapter 4
1. *De Consideratione ad Eugenium in Cistercian Fathers*, vol. 37, trans. J. O. Anderson and E. T. Kennan (Kalamazoo, 1976).

Chapter 5
1. Quoted in David Clutterbuck and Stuart Crainer, *Makers of Management: Men and Women Who Changed the Business World* (Guild Publishing, 1990).
2. *Leadership Skills*, John Adair (Chartered Institute of Personnel and Development, 1997).
3. 'The Bases of Social Power', in *Studies in Social Power*, French, J. and Raven, B. (Institute for Social Research, 1959).
4. *The Situational Leader*, Paul Hersey (Center for Leadership Studies, 1997).
5. *The Seven Habits of Highly Effective People*, Stephen Covey (Simon & Schuster, 1992).

Chapter 13
1. *Understanding Leadership*, John Finney (Daybreak, 1989).
2. *Transforming Leadership*, Richard Higginson (SPCK, 1996).
3. MBTI and Myers-Briggs Type Indicator are the registered UK and US trade marks of Consulting Psychologists Press, Inc. Oxford Psychologists Press is the exclusive licensee of the trade marks in the UK.
4. *Navigating Complexity*, Arthur Bartram (The Industrial Society, 1999).
5. *Employability – Your Way to Career Success*, Susan Bloch and Terence Bates (Kogan Page/AMED, 1995).
6. *Independent on Sunday*, 11 February 2001.
7. Employer of the Year 2000 Awards.
8. DfEE *Case Studies in a Changing World* (www.dti.gov.uk/work-lifebalance)

Chapter 14
1. *Dialogues of Gregory the Great, The Life of Saint Benedict*, Adalbert de Vogné (St Bede's Publication, 1993).

Chapter 16
1. *How to Choose Your Next Employer*, Robert Herman (Oakhill, 2000); www.herman.net/articles

Appendix:
Key Business Themes from the
Rule of St Benedict

Subject	Ref.	Quotation
Decision-making	3.13	If you act always after hearing the counsel of others, you will avoid the need to repent of your decision afterwards.
Hospitality	53.1	All guests who present themselves are to be welcomed as Christ.
Humility	7.31	... whenever one of us is raised to a position of prominence there is always an element of pride involved ...
Integrity	19.7	When we sing in choir there is complete harmony between the things in our minds and the meaning of the words we sing.
Leadership principles	2.39	By encouraging through their faithful ministry better standards for those in their care, they will develop higher ideals in their own lives.
	2	The task of the Abbot is to adapt with understanding to the needs of each.
Leadership style	2.25	Use now the encouragement of a loving parent and now the threats of a harsh disciplinarian.
	64.9	The Abbot must understand that the call of their office is not to exercise power over those who are their subjects but to serve and help them in their needs.
	64.19	Manage everything in the monastery so that the strong may have ideals to inspire them and the weak may not be frightened away by excessive demands.
Life/work balance Tolerance	Pro 46	We hope to set down nothing harsh and nothing burdensome. The good of all concerned prompts us to a little strictness in order to rectify faults.
	24.1	The severity of the punishment should correspond to the gravity of the fault committed.
	40.6	Agree to drink in moderation and not until we are full.
Lifelong learning	73	We can only blush with shame when we reflect on the negligence and inadequacy of the lives we lead.
	Pro 45	We mean to establish a school for the Lord's service.

Subject	Ref.	Quotation
Personal development	Pro 6	For we must at all times use the good gifts he has given us.
	Pro 15	Who is there with a love of true life and a longing for days of real fulfilment?
Relationships	30.1	There is a proper way of dealing with every age and every degree of understanding and we should find the right way of dealing with the young.
	72.3	They should try to be the first to show respect to one another with the greatest patience in tolerating weaknesses of body or character.
	34.5	Those who do not need as much as some others should thank God for the strength they have been given and not be sorry for themselves. Those who need more should be humble about their weaknesses and not become self-important in enjoying the indulgence granted them.
Retirement and recruitment	37.1	Human nature itself is drawn to the tender concern for those in the extremes of age and youth, but the authority of the Rule should reinforce this natural instinct.
Time management	Pro 13	Run while you have the light of life before the darkness of death overtakes you.
	4.44	Keep the reality of death always before your eyes and have a care about how you act every hour of your life.
	4.48 & 19.1	God is present everywhere.
	Pro 43	While we still have the time in this mortal life and the opportunity to fulfil what God asks of us through a life guided by his light we must hurry forward and act in a way that will bring blessings in eternal life.
	43.2	Nothing is to be accounted more important than the word of God.
	48.1	Idleness is the enemy of the soul.
Importance of a vision	3.6	It is just as important for the Superior to be far-sighted and fair in administration.
Wisdom	7.61	The wise we should remember are to be recognized in words that are few.
Working in teams	35.1	Everyone in the community should take turns serving in the kitchen and at table.
	22.8	Each should give encouragement to those who are sleepy and given to making excuses for being late.
	31.14	. . . a kindly word is of greater value than a gift, however precious.
	38.6	Everyone in the community should be attentive to the needs of their neighbours as they eat and drink so that there should be no need for anyone to ask for what they require.
	40.9	Above all else . . . there should be no murmuring in the community.